ABOUT THE AUTHOR

Forty years after he'd discovered QPR, the club retains its near total control on Simon's life. In 2003, at just 36 years of age, Simon was diagnosed with Parkinson's disease. Not even this degenerative neurological illness could affect his total commitment to Queens Park Rangers. Yet again, the 2015-2016 campaign saw Simon and his son Joshua renew their season tickets, all but guaranteeing another 9 months of stomach churning, high octane twists and turns by a club that always seem to test the nerves of their supporters.

Many thanks to Don Mammatt for his fantastic book cover. The iconic No. 10 shirt will bring back so many happy memories for QPR fans of a certain vintage.

Many thanks to Queens Park Rangers for their programme images and crests.

Simon Ingram

QPR Away Day Travels

Copyright © Simon Ingram (2017)

The right of Simon Ingram to be identified as author of this work has been asserted by him in accordance with section 77 and 78 of the Copyright, Designs and Patents Act 1988.

All rights reserved. No part of this publication may be reproduced, stored in a retrieval system, or transmitted in any form or by any means, electronic, mechanical, photocopying, recording, or otherwise, without the prior permission of the publishers.

Any person who commits any unauthorized act in relation to this publication may be liable to criminal prosecution and civil claims for damages.

A CIP catalogue record for this title is available from the British Library.

ISBN 9781786299192 (Paperback)
ISBN 9781786299208 (Hardback)
ISBN 9781786299215 (eBook)

www.austinmacauley.com

First Published (2017)
Austin Macauley Publishers Ltd.
25 Canada Square
Canary Wharf
London
E14 5LQ

COME ON YOU SUPER-HOOPS, 1975

When, as a youngster, I discovered the world of football, I instantly became a hopeless case.

With the destructive powers of a hurricane, football took total control of my life. Anything not connected to 'footie' was simply blown away.

Within a matter of weeks, and with a final twist of the knife, I became a fan of a small West London club… Queens Park Rangers. Having said that, there is a small part of me that truly believes that in some cases you are selected as a supporter, not the other way around. Certainly, I think that if there is such a thing as a guardian angel guiding individuals through life, mine has a wicked sense of humour!

Over the next 40 years, QPR would shamelessly go on to take my money and break my heart throughout the months of August to May. How many people can honestly say that as a ten-year-old they sat in the living room of their family home over the Christmas holiday wearing their team's colours as if it would influence the day's football results? I can!

Only football fans of a certain vintage can possibly know how devastating it felt to have tuned in to the old BBC Radio 2 Saturday afternoon sports programme to learn of yet another defeat suffered by their team. The poor, crackly reception and the almost apologetic voice of James Alexander Gordon when broadcasting the final scores at 5pm would make or break the remainder of my weekend.

This book is my attempt to help redress the balance, offering an insight into the fun, the laughs and the enjoyment of being a fan of QPR FC since the mid-1970s.

QPR – Away Day Travels is intended to be a travel companion, something to help ease the boredom of the many hours of long distance journeys, although it really does not matter if you read a page a night to help ease your sleep!

You will read my own match reports from 'classic' encounters over the years, as well as a potted history of the club from the last five decades. In short, I am hoping there's something for everyone.

Although this is a book about my 40 years of being a QPR fan, much of its content will be easily understood by all football fanatics. I can only hope this book does our story justice.

INTRODUCTION

I'm assuming there are lots of people who, like me, enjoy taking the occasional nostalgic look back at their lives. Perhaps something a little less common is one of the causes for my trips down memory lane… football.

As a 9 year-old boy, the instantaneous and profound changes to my life brought about by my discovery of the 'beautiful game' mean I have much to thank it for. It made me new friends, kept me active and perhaps most importantly of all, it has given me the drive and determination to be the best I could possibly be when facing up to lots of challenges that life has thrown at me.

Sadly, for me, this limitless enthusiasm didn't spill over into my years at school. I left it incredibly late before I finally put in sufficient effort to achieve 'O' Level passes in Maths, English and Science.

Whereas my poor return on the years invested in the UK's education system mean my writing will always be a little clumsy, I sincerely hope you find *QPR – Away Day Travels* to be an interesting and enjoyable read.

QUEENS PARK RANGERS F.C.

Queens Park Rangers is a small club from West London that few people really know about or understand. The passion and dedication felt for the team by its supporters more than makes up for any lack of numbers.

Home or away, over the years QPR fans have regularly created an atmosphere that even players from the very top of English football have found incredibly difficult to cope with.

Its capacity may be a little under 18,500, however, when Loftus Road is full, the fans create a buzz unlike anything I've ever experienced at any other football ground. Such is the vibrancy of the place, when it's bouncing, there's nowhere for players to hide. It's almost as if you can see the colour draining from the faces of the opposition.

Having visited the completely rebuilt Wembley Stadium in May 2014, I'm pleased to confirm that QPR fans are more than capable of transporting that superb atmosphere from Loftus Road to one of the world's top stadiums.

PROLOGUE

I discovered football shortly after celebrating my 9th birthday. Within weeks, my life had been totally transformed; the speed and scale of those changes significantly increased by something as plain and simple as a blue and green football playing card.

Updated on many occasions over the years and still popular with the youngsters of today, back in the mid-1970s the playing cards came with a flat, almost inedible piece of chewing gum. Pale yellow in colour, with the look (and probably taste) of a small piece of plastic from a self-assembly Airfix scale model toy of the day.

The playing cards would be held between two fingers and flicked towards the straight edge base of a wall. The card closest to the wall would win all of the other cards in play.

Another method for exchanging cards was a straightforward trade, most transactions being completed at school before the start of each of the morning and afternoon lessons.

The playing card that had such a dramatic effect on the rest of my life was Stan Bowles of QPR. A player and a team totally unknown to me at the time.

Football had taken over my life, from that moment on I became a lost cause, immediately collecting the rest of the Queens Park Rangers playing cards. I remember in particular being really impressed that one of the QPR players, Gerry Francis, was the captain of England. I was hooked!

The buzz I got from football couldn't have been any greater, even if someone had plugged me directly into the national power grid. I simply couldn't get enough of the stuff. Playing, watching, and even talking about the game. I simply came alive when being close to anything connected with football, especially anything to do with QPR.

My 49th birthday is not so many months away, and as if just to prove. I'm still totally fixated by the game; I'm sitting here on Monday, 15th

December 2014, watching QPR being soundly beaten by Everton. We've just conceded our third goal and yet again this season we're playing like a team who don't belong in the top tier of English football.

Just like the youngster who started to follow QPR way back in 1975, I still believe my team should win every game they play. Perhaps this may make it a little easier to understand when I say I still find it incredibly difficult to sit and watch my team get thrashed.

In an attempt to ease the pain in what is looking increasingly like we could be on the way to heavy defeat, I've decided to sit and work on this, my latest book.

As for tonight's game against Everton, we would eventually go on to lose 3-1.

The defeat soon placed firmly behind me, I can again focus on trying to explain to you, the reader, exactly what it means to support a small, unfashionable club from West London: Queens Park Rangers FC.

Loftus Road
The Home of Queens Park Rangers FC

Loftus Road Stadium, London - Shepherd's Bush by seitentasche

Stan Bowles, instrumental in my becoming a QPR supporter.

CONTENTS

Chapter 1	*QPR – The Rollercoaster Ride*
Chapter 2	*On The Road*
Chapter 3	*Cup Competitions*
Chapter 4	*1970s*
Chapter 5	*1980s*
Chapter 6	*A Potted History – 1990 to 2015*
	Away Day Travels
Chapter 7	*May 10th 2015*

CHAPTER 1
QPR - THE ROLLERCOASTER RIDE

Feeding my addiction of supporting QPR over the years has given me first-hand experience of the twists and turns in the club's fortunes; supporters like me are often left feeling elated or angry and, if I'm honest, more than a little nauseous.

Throughout its erratic day-to-day existence, it's true to say that although I've remained a steadfastly loyal fan, QPR and I haven't always been the best of friends. My patience with the club I've followed since the autumn of 1975 has been severely tested by numerous monumental on-the-pitch failures. For example, who could forget in November 2002, the painful and humiliating exit from the FA Cup at the hands of non-league Vauxhall Motors? QPR lost 3-4 on penalties, something made all the more miserable as my long-suffering wife works at Vauxhall's UK Headquarters in Luton.

Unbelievably in 1993, just 9 years prior to that most humbling of defeats, the Super Hoops had finished as London's top club in the Premiership, ending the season in a highly respectable 5th place. The capital's more 'glamorous' clubs, Arsenal, Tottenham, Chelsea etc., couldn't match our performances and subsequent points tally that season.

Indeed, the 1992-1993 campaign proved to be an excellent time to be a QPR fan. Ex-England and QPR Captain Gerry Francis had come back to the club to become manager, and had shaped a team that in its day could take on and beat anyone in the division.

The meteoric free fall down through the football leagues in the mid-1990s and early 2000s was breath taking. So rapid was our fall from grace that at one point it seemed we might end up dropping into the fourth tier of English football - or worse, due to the financial problems gripping the club - we could simply go out of business.

Perhaps most embarrassing of all though, were the actions of the owners or senior members of staff who seemed to thrive on making headlines in many of the daily newspapers; our once proud club was dragged through a series of almost unbelievable episodes, turning us into the laughing stock of English football.

Fortunately, for me, a mixture of blind faith and eternal optimism kept me supporting the Super Hoops.

Now back in the Premiership following the 1-0 victory over Derby County in the 2013/2014 Wembley Stadium Playoff Final last May, I think it's fair to say the rollercoaster ride continues.

There's no doubt about it, following QPR is hard work. Certainly the difficulty of supporting the club through thick and thin can often be a painful experience; take today as a classic example. It's Saturday 21st February 2015, and QPR are playing away at Hull City. Both teams are hovering too close to the relegation zone for comfort. In typical QPR fashion, we have had to make things incredibly difficult for ourselves by playing the majority of the game with 10 men; with Joey Barton being sent off early in the first half. A spirited performance from QPR saw us heading for a 1-1 draw until, in a script all too familiar to QPR fans, Hull City scored in the last few minutes to win the game 2-1.

Even allowing for this seemingly never-ending series of disappointments, my book *'QPR – Away Day Travels'* is far removed from anything resembling a hatchet job on the Super Hoops. For me, that would be like criticising an old friend, something I'd struggle to do with any enthusiasm. Although that's not to say I haven't become extremely vocal when questioning lots of seemingly bizarre decisions made by endless players and managers over the years.

It hasn't all been bad though: FA Cup Finals, League Cup Finals, even reaching the Quarter Finals of the UEFA Cup! All this, along with promotion to the Premier League, achieved by a small club from West London.

I'll never forget seeing QPR being led out at Wembley Stadium, although sadly, I'm yet to experience a cup final victory! Something that most fans would agree won't be happening any time soon as we've struggled to get past the cup competition's preliminary rounds in recent times.

It really doesn't matter if you are a QPR fan or not, I'm hoping that by reading this book you will begin to appreciate, and perhaps understand, just some of the events that have helped make my years of supporting Queens Park Rangers football club so varied and wide ranging.

Despite the fact that *'QPR – Away Day Travels'* is a look back at the last 40 years of following QPR, please note, it is not intended to be a definitive and detailed historical account of our club from 1975 to date. It's more of a summary of the last 5 decades from a fan's perspective. Something that perhaps would score you a few points if, after reading it, you took 'QPR, 1975 to 2015' as a 'Specialised Subject' on the BBC's long running 'Mastermind' television programme.

I've already stated it really doesn't matter if you read a page a night to help you sleep or if, as originally intended, you take it with you as part of a group when travelling to away fixtures. It's something to be read and to hopefully promote memories from years gone by.

The most important thing though is, whatever your circumstances, you feel a little of the magic that exists when following football, especially Queens Park Rangers FC.

CHAPTER 2

ON THE ROAD

Travelling to away fixtures can be a cramped and uncomfortable affair. The early excitement of spending time away with your family and friends following QPR in unfamiliar surroundings is quickly followed by mind numbing boredom as you pass mile after mile of orange and white traffic cones choking our nation's motorway network.

Anyone unfortunate enough to use the heavily congested roads in this country can't have failed to notice these small, brightly coloured barriers. Used to great effect to calm and direct the flow of traffic, occasionally they also appear to restrict the progress of travellers on perfectly good sections of road. It's so frustrating having to sit stationery in your vehicle, nose to tail in a traffic jam separated from clean, clear carriageway just inches away.

This is in no way an attempt to single out a particular team or location for criticism, but for me the journey through Birmingham is nothing short of depressing. Travelling northbound on the M6 Motorway, just past the beautiful old Fort Dunlop building, row after row of electricity transformers buzz 24/7 highlighting the aggressive and urgent push to supply the region's rapidly growing industrial manufacturing requirements in years gone by. I'm assuming that the cost of replacing the infrastructure with a more environmentally friendly, 21st century version is prohibitive, meaning there's no immediate plans to upgrade.

It doesn't take a tremendous amount of effort or indeed creative thinking to lift the spirits of the travelling fans. Usually, once the decision has been made to pull over at the next available services, the magic of the day returns in an instant, especially when someone has remembered to bring along a football!

Over the years, the younger members of the party have run off steam on the smallest of grassed areas at any number of refreshment facilities dotted around the country while the adults stand in line for a hot drink. This is something we've actively encouraged (with adult supervision of course!) as I can still remember as a youngster the importance I attached to kicking a ball around on a Saturday with my mates. I was so proud of my first QPR football kit, I honestly think when I was wearing it (all the time!) I'd put in so much more effort trying to emulate the skill and effort of my QPR heroes of the day (Gerry Francis, Stan Bowles etc.)

Another football top that had the same effect was the 1970s classic England 'Admiral' shirt. Again, with six QPR players in the England squad of the day I could pretend I was Gerry Francis, Stan Bowles etc. What a fantastic time to be a QPR supporter!

Back to our travels, having stopped at a service station for refreshments. Who'd have thought that a group of football fans, some daring to fly in the face of popular fashion advice by wearing replica shirts of their chosen team, could stand in the queue next to the great and the good of society, waiting patiently for their ridiculously overpriced Mocha-Chocca-Latte without breaking into a full-blown rendition of "Here we go, here we go, here we go"? Amazing.

I'm joking of course, but I believe it's just possible that companies looking to reduce spend against their training budgets could promote a better team building ethic within their organisations by using the bonding influence of football travel as a cheaper alternative. For the price of match-day tickets, a hot drink and a bag of chips, any employer seeking to get individuals working as a cohesive unit could perhaps consider this as an option.

The format is pretty straightforward; simply provide tickets and the keys to a seven-seater vehicle to as many groups of 3 employees as required. The only rules would be that the vehicles should start the journey and arrive at the destination together. The tickets should be for three sets of two members of the same family, ideally a parent and child partnership, and finally, the journey time would have to last a minimum of two hours.

If the group is anything like the one I travel in, tensions will start to rise the second that members of the party are late for the agreed departure time!

Once the journey has started, in my experience, by the time you've all agreed that the time is right to pull into a service station you'll have a mixture of people bursting for the toilet, starving, thirsty or just in need of stretching their legs for 10 minutes. All the time though, there's a constant need for diplomacy or the whole thing would simply fall apart.

Our band of travelling supporters is small in number, with Terry Cadby, Lee Edmonds and I being joined by a new recruit, Lloyd Bailey way back in the early 1990s. Whereas Terry, Lee and I had been at school together from the age of 9 to 16, Lloyd joined the three amigos courtesy of us all playing for the same Sunday League football team: Cosworth FC.

Lloyd has been a fairly consistent traveller since 1992, funny to think then that even after some 23 years, he's still considered the 'new boy'. It's almost as if we've adopted rural village rules, where anyone who hadn't been around for more than a set number of years is 'new' to the area. The trouble is, the set number of years is a moving target!

Our number has doubled in the last few years with the arrival of Teddy Cadby, Henry Edmonds, Matthew Bailey and finally my son, Joshua Ingram. We all support QPR and ultimately want to see our team win, that's where the similarities end though.

We are a fine band of travelling buddies although some key parts of our personalities are at completely opposite ends of the social spectrum.

In amongst our party we have control freaks, easy going laugh-a-minute individuals, fast food lovers, health fanatics and finally fans who look as if supporting Queens Park Rangers has placed the weight of the world on their shoulders.

Fortunately for us, the regular travelling companions have known each other for many, many years. We are without doubt all well past the stage of worrying about overly upsetting one another. My two closest friends, Terry Cadby and Lee Edmonds, are complete opposite personalities, with me fitting in somewhere in the middle. Perhaps that's why we've been friends for so long.

Before I move on to the next chapter I have to include a short piece on how a car full of football fans feel the need to carry-out an 'in-car' assessment on your performance as the designated driver, something I've noticed that gets steadily more critical and vocal the older the passengers get.

A great example of this comes from our journey home following a visit to Loftus Road where we had Terry's dad, Dave Cadby and Lee's dad, Eric Edmonds, squeezed into the car with us. Two lifelong QPR supporters and a couple of fantastic fellas, until that is, you have them offering their 'advice' from the back seat.

They proved to be an early sort of unhelpful satellite navigation system, frustratingly though, one that couldn't be switched-off!

Most of the journey to and from Loftus Road was accompanied by endless pearls of wisdom coming from our two senior R's, such as

"Overtake that idiot" or pointing out of the window in what could have been an observation aimed at any number of individuals going about their daily business. "Mind this bloke Simon, he doesn't know what he's doing" or my own personal favourite, in these days of averaging speed cameras on every stretch of motorway under repair, "Get your foot down Simon, for Christ's sake."

My only respite came when Lee and Terry had heard enough from their respective fathers, letting go with a torrent of 'advice' of their own, often liberally sprinkled with a few choice expletives for good measure.

The situation came to a head on the journey home late one evening when the A406 (North Circular) had been dug up for urgent repairs. The carriageway had been reduced to a single lane with a maximum speed of 30mph. The bottleneck often caused when a large number of vehicles join an already busy stretch of road often turns the surrounding network into nothing more than a massive car park. Whereas over the years I have learned that just to keep moving, even at a speed well below the permitted level, is a real sign of progress, clearly not everyone in the car that night shared this view.

We'd only travelled a short distance, some 200 metres or so, when suddenly at a level well above the buzz of the normal post-match excitable chatter, Dave shouted "TURN RIGHT!" Instantly the inside of the car fell silent, in a safety manoeuvre that any driving test examiner would have given me top marks for, I spotted a gap in the cones and thinking there was an imminent risk of a collision, I took the immediate right-hand turn.

There was no time to relax though as another barked order came from the back seat, "TURN LEFT!" and this time from the usually mild-mannered Eric Edmonds. I felt like it was turning into a sort of geriatric version of a scene from one of the many action-packed "Fast and Furious" films; I spotted a gap in the sea of cones, and swung the car to the left.

Then, to my acute embarrassment, in what proved to be more 'Keystone Cops' than Vin Diesel, I realised that we'd come to a halt in one of the bays set aside for the fleet of service vehicles busily carrying out the repairs to the pot holed road surface.

I sat in utter disbelief when both Dave and Eric leaned forward and asked, "Simon, what did you do that for?" Priceless!

Lesson learned, I now understand that when it comes to travelling, the senior R's tend to suffer from a sort of Tourette's syndrome. Whereas the advice they give is always well intentioned, it is most definitely to be ignored.

CHAPTER 3

CUP COMPETITIONS

I simply love to write, not that I'm saying that *'QPR – Away Day Travels'* is going to be a classic read. I'll be happy if I can get across just a little of the magic felt by a small group of fans, spending time watching their team travelling up and down the English football leagues.

Unlike the teams who regularly look to finish in one of the top four places in the Premier League, qualifying for the following season's Champions League competition, QPR fans never know for sure that we will beat anyone. A fine performance against one of the bigger teams in the league is often followed by a run of poor results.

Most fans following an English football club fully accept that qualifying for the Champion's League is something that simply isn't going to happen. Although like many fans supporting 'ordinary' clubs, I do have an opinion on this competition.

I genuinely feel that the format of the Champion's League is wrong. Even calling it the Champion's League is misleading as in my opinion, what's Champion about finishing 2nd, 3rd or 4th? So, please start calling it what it is, The European League. Be careful though, are you sure that you want to proceed with your thinly veiled plan? I'm confident that football in this country would continue without the fab-four highly polished elite teams, but could they survive without us, the teams that make up 80% of the current Premier League? I suspect the answer to that is a resounding 'NO' as in my opinion it's all a question of money. The fabulous stadia that have been built over the last 10 years need to be full of fans every other Saturday for a nine-month season. Look at the Manchester City example, playing against Champion's League opposition at the Etihad in 2014, the stadium nowhere close to being full.

One final word of warning, we already have an example of a once seemingly untouchable cup competition waning in popularity, albeit a domestic trophy: the FA Cup.

Maybe it's just me, but I can't seem to shake the feeling that there are powerful people, and organisations, who appear to be focused on short term income rather than the long term good of football in this country.

It's probably me getting old and a little cynical, but am I really the only one to spot a possible connection between the reduced sparkle of the FA Cup and Manchester United's temporary withdrawal from the competition in 1999? The apparent decision to favour taking part in an unproven competition with limited appeal in England (the World Club Cup) over the prestigious FA Cup tournament is a difficult one to understand. Certainly for someone who supports a club some way away from qualifying for the competition!

The devastating blow felt by the FA (Cup) after Manchester United's temporary withdrawal is something that in my opinion still affects the competition today. I'm not talking about income, as I'm sure revenues are up year-on-year as the clamour for big businesses to be connected with football appears as strong as ever. I'm talking about the prestige of a once mighty cup competition being damaged with there apparently being no quick fix.

Ultimately, it would appear that the desire of many clubs to progress past the preliminary rounds and progress to the Wembley final has significantly diminished in recent years. Indeed, some of the top clubs routinely field a number of reserve team players, especially for the competition's early rounds.

In years gone by, the world stopped when the FA Cup Final was being played. Always 3pm on the Saturday following the final match of the domestic season, shown live on the BBC and ITV Television Channels.

I still remember the strength of feeling generated by the FA Cup Final and the utter, almost crushing elation placed on individuals fortunate enough to score the winning goal. Two players in particular spring to mind: Bobby Stokes (1976, Southampton v Manchester United) and Roger Osbourne (1978, Ipswich Town v Arsenal). Sadly, both of these players would never again reach such a high in their football careers. After scoring his goal, Osbourne in particular looked to be a totally spent force, almost unable to walk. It may sound a little daft, but in my opinion, Osbourne never really recovered from the incredible high of beating Arsenal in the early May sunshine at Wembley Stadium. Sadly, he'd only feature in a handful of matches for the club after picking up an FA Cup winner's medal.

Such was the interest in the final itself, the BBC broadcast a special programme the night before the game to talk about every aspect of the following day's match.

It was so very different for the 2014 Final though (Arsenal v Hull). The match had the feel of being shoehorned into a convenient slot in between regular league games nominated by the satellite channel at a time and date to keep their viewing figures at a premium. How very sad.

CHAPTER 4
1970s

The only sensible place to start this chapter is to name the QPR team that began the 1975-76 campaign:

1. Phil Parkes
2. Dave Clement
3. Ian Gillard
4. John Hollins
5. Frank McLintock
6. Dave Webb
7. Dave Thomas
8. Gerry Francis
9. Don Masson
10. Stan Bowles
11. Don Givens
Sub: Mick Leach
Manager: Dave Sexton

The QPR team for the 1975-1976 season was a great one, full of quality, skill and confidence. Class ran through the entire side, most of the playing staff already had, or would go on to represent their country at international level during their time at QPR.

Dave Sexton, the QPR Manager, had timed the preparation for the 1975-76 season to perfection. The players were obviously firing on all cylinders as a few weeks before the first game of the English domestic season the Super Hoops took part in a pre-season tour of West Germany. In the most unexpected of results, QPR simply brushed aside the Bundesliga champions, Borussia Mönchengladbach 1-4, a sign of things to come.

16th August 1975 – on a hot, sunny afternoon at the height of summer, in the days before all-seater stadia, a crowd of over 27,000 squeezed into Loftus Road to watch QPR tear into their opening day opponents, Liverpool FC.

The football produced by QPR was simply breathtaking. Indeed, the opening goal of the game scored by the QPR and England Captain, Gerry Francis, went on to win that season's 'Match of the Day' Goal of the Season competition.

Thanks to YouTube, I've watched this wonderfully crafted goal on many occasions. A beautiful example of passing and movement, Don Masson, Don Givens, Stan Bowles and finally Gerry Francis carved open the central spine of the Liverpool team. The move finished off with a clinical shot into the corner of the net, leaving the England goalkeeper, Ray Clemence, with no chance.

A second goal followed, this time scored by an unsung Rangers hero, Mick Leach. The match finished 2-0, QPR simply purring to victory against the Anfield Reds.

A result made all the more impressive when you consider that less than two years later, 8 of the Liverpool team starting that day would go on to overcome the West German champions in Liverpool's first European Cup Final victory on a monumental night in the Italian capital, Rome. Goals from Terry McDermott, Tommy Smith and Phil Neal secured a deserved 3-1 win.

Over the course of the 75-76 season, many more victories were to follow as our opponents struggled to cope with the 90-minute onslaught from this quality QPR team. Home or away, this free-flowing Rangers side put many teams to the sword. On our day we were irrepressible, victories against Everton (5-0), Tottenham (3-0) and Manchester United (1-0) would be recorded. Perhaps the most impressive of all though, QPR thrashed Derby County, the current league champions 1-5 at the Baseball Ground, with Stan Bowles taking home the match ball after scoring a hat-trick.

Sadly, QPR's challenge for the title would come off the rails in mid-April 1976. A 3-2 loss away to Norwich City would prove to be the game that cost us the title…This game is featured in far greater detail later on in this book.

Despite the mostly lean times since the mighty Super Hoops finished just behind the eventual champions Liverpool, my total fascination for the team from West London remains undiminished.

For a time in the mid-1970s, QPR adopted a style of play first mastered by the Dutch national team that so nearly won them the World Cup in 1974. A hugely entertaining style of football that sadly went unrewarded as just like the Dutch, QPR would go on to finish the 1975-76 season in second place. In a cruel twist of fate, QPR lost by a single point to Liverpool, the team they'd totally outplayed and beaten some nine months before.

Playing such an entertaining style of football won six QPR players England call-ups. Off the field too, QPR players found that their individual successes were giving them wider appeal.

Phil Parkes (Goalkeeper), found himself advertising Cossack Hairspray, whereas the mercurial talents of Stan Bowles earned him a place on the 1970s Superstars television programme.

'Superstars' was legendary for being tough on athletes right across the world of sport. Does anyone else remember the British Judo Champion Brian Jacks? I seem to remember him eating his way through a ton of fruit during the two days of filming for the 1-hour TV show, claiming it gave him added strength. This may be correct as his greatest triumph came about in the gymnasium. Demonstrating a huge amount of upper body strength, he set an all-time record for the number of arm dips completed on the parallel bars.

Our Stan didn't exactly excel in any of the challenges, although his low point probably came about midway through the competition during the Pistol Shooting. Already too far away from being able to catch the leader, Stan made absolutely sure of continuing his poor points tally by being disqualified; instead of shooting the target he blasted a hole in the table immediately in front of where he stood!

This is just one example of the wonderfully unique playing staff at Loftus Road during the mid-1970s that made supporting QPR so addictive.

The six QPR and England internationals (Left to Right): Dave Thomas, Stan Bowles, Gerry Francis, Phil Parkes, Ian Gillard and the late Dave Clement

The six includes Dave Clement (not shown)

Although our style of football remained entertaining, the following season (1976-77) proved far more difficult for QPR. Wins that a few months before seemed to come easily now had to be ground out. Indeed, our opponents for the opening game of the new season, Everton FC, had been demolished by QPR the previous season 5-0. Unbelievably, the score this time around was a resounding 0-4 victory for the visitors.

Indeed, it took us four attempts to secure our first victory that season, on 4th September 1976. Coincidently this was my first ever visit to Loftus Road.

QPR 1 - 0 WBA
(SATURDAY 4TH SEPTEMBER 1976)

The whole event was a mind-numbingly excitable occasion, although it seemed that I was awake on the hour every hour throughout the night before the big game. When morning finally arrived, I felt as if I could have run all the way to London.

I had just turned 10 years of age, the thought of travelling to Loftus Road to see the mighty QPR play left me feeling intoxicated, the blood in my veins laced with enough adrenaline to make an elephant dance.

My parents never got anywhere close to understanding my total obsession with football, if I'd have tried to explain why I had become totally fixated with QPR the conversation would still be going on today. Whereas I'm the first to admit that when it comes to all matters QPR I'm a complete basket case, I think my parents were hoping that my addiction was a passing phase! Therefore, it's probably no surprise to anyone when I say that my first trip to Loftus Road was with another family: the O'Briens.

The O'Briens had moved to Northampton from London's Shepherds Bush some two years earlier. Staunch QPR supporters and great company, making them the ideal people to accompany me on my first trip to Loftus Road.

With the QPR connection, John and Shirley's son Kevin and I were always going to be friends, the fact that we played for the same Under-13 local football team sealed the deal.

The match itself was far from being a classic encounter. The free-flowing football that tore so many teams apart just a few months before was seemingly replaced by a more cautious and methodical game plan. Probably as a result of opposition managers and back-room staff doing their homework on how to play against QPR, picking the players and tactics necessary to stifle the flair and creativity regularly used by the Super Hoops to dominate matches just a few months before.

Of course the loss of the QPR and England Captain, Gerry Francis, for almost the entire season through injury, came as a massive blow. Without his influence, the brilliant QPR side of the 1975-76 season seemed to lose drive and determination, in short, we'd lost the player who could and often did make a difference.

The QPR Manager, Dave Sexton, clearly knew we needed a temporary replacement. The man selected for the job was Arsenal's Eddie Kelly.

Although he'd signed for QPR before the match against WBA, it was too late for him to make his debut.

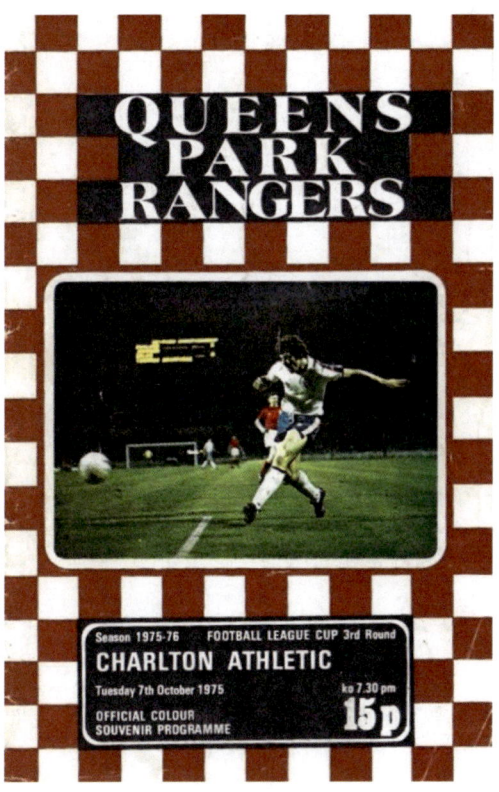

Ian Gillard on international duty

I know this may seem a little unkind but in my opinion, Kelly looked too old and too fat to adequately plug the temporary gap in our midfield. In short, it didn't work.

Even without Francis, QPR would still go on to secure a 1-0 victory against newly promoted WBA. In truth an instantly forgettable fixture, the visitors offering little in the way of desire and invention. The only high point proved to be Ian Gillard's well taken goal, a bullet of a header whistling passed the WBA Goalkeeper.

The QPR and England No. 3 had timed his run into the penalty box to perfection, meeting a cross in from the right hand side unchallenged giving him plenty of time to steady himself before scoring. Ian Gillard was a tremendous servant to QPR. I believe he proved to be the last of the playing staff from the great 75-76 side to leave the club. Most definitely an unsung hero, the fact that he remained at Loftus Road and played under so many managers during his career means that in my opinion, he is one of the first names on my Rangers Legends team sheet. Thanks to him, my very first visit to Loftus Road will live long in the memory.

From the moment the massive club crest came into view as I climbed the steps of the Loftus Road stand, I knew the day was going to be a special one. The camaraderie felt with the thousands of other fans shuffling along the concrete walkways as they made their way to their 'patch' on the terracing is best described as tribal.

Shortly before kick-off the passion and expectation levels rise, people who've never been to a football match before clearly feel the 'buzz' when visiting Loftus Road. This adrenaline fuelled 'rush' is heightened by the tight and compact nature of the stadium. The feeling of being able to reach out and touch the players adds to the spectacular atmosphere.

Before the introduction of all-seater stadiums, a QPR v Leeds Utd. fixture in April 1974 attracted a record 35,353 fans. Perhaps, somewhat mercifully and for the safety of all those concerned, QPR lost the match 0-1. I can only guess at the atmosphere that day and the level of carnage had we scored.

Late in 2010, shortly before the highly-charged Championship encounter with Cardiff City, I'd arranged for a thank you message to be broadcast to John and Kevin on the electronic screen that now sits on the roof of the School End stand. After many years away from Loftus Road John and Kevin were due to join a group of us to watch the game. Sadly, for health reasons John was unable to travel to the game with Kevin.

Despite a good run in the UEFA Cup and League Cup competitions that season, the forward thinking and hugely respected QPR Manager, Dave Sexton was tempted away from Loftus Road by Manchester United in the summer of 1977.

Initially, QPR tried to promote from within, with Frank Sibley taking control of managing the club. Sadly, in my opinion, someone pressed the panic button a little too quickly and the team that finished in second place just three seasons before was broken up and sold. Inevitably, the players brought in weren't the same quality as the players they were replacing, and QPR were relegated from Division 1 at the end of the 1978-79 season. The QPR manager who took the club into Division Two (Steve Burtenshaw) was sacked. Someone was needed to rebuild the team and begin the task of getting the club back into the First Division. The man chosen: Tommy Docherty.

He was thought to be an odd choice in some quarters as he'd already held the managerial post at QPR for a period of 28 days in 1968. A serious disagreement with the club's owner, Jim Gregory, brought his first spell in charge to an end in less than a month.

It's rumoured that on taking charge in May of 1979, Docherty introduced himself to the players, telling them that they should trust him. Stan Bowles, QPR's star player of the time instantly got himself banished to the reserves by saying that he'd sooner trust KFC's (Kentucky Fried Chicken) Colonel Sanders with his chickens!

Docherty busied himself in the transfer market, the first 6 months of his reign saw the arrival of several high-profile players, including:

Chris Woods (Forest)
Tony Currie (Leeds)
Bobby Hazell (Wolves)
Steve Wicks (Derby)
Also some players for the future, including:
Gary Micklewhite (Man Utd.)
Steve Burke (Forest)

The opening game of the 1979-1980 season saw the talented QPR striking partnership of Clive Allen and Paul Goddard both open their goal scoring accounts for the season. A crowd of just over 12,500 people saw QPR beat Bristol Rovers 2-0.

COME ON YOU SUPER HOOPS!

		Home					Away			
P	W	D	L	F	A	W	D	L	F	A	Pts

(Division II table, 17 games played)

Team	P	W	D	L	F	A	W	D	L	F	A	Pts
QPR	17	7	1	1	26	6	3	2	3	8	9	23
Chlsea	17	5	1	2	12	7	6	0	3	17	13	23
Nwcstl	17	7	1	0	13	5	2	4	3	10	10	23
Luton	17	4	4	1	17	8	4	2	2	13	9	22
Lcstr C	17	5	2	2	15	11	3	4	1	16	10	22
Brghm	17	5	2	1	10	5	4	2	3	13	12	22
W Hm	17	6	1	2	13	5	3	1	4	7	11	20
Sndlnd	17	8	1	0	22	6	0	2	6	3	14	19
Ntts C	17	4	3	2	15	9	3	1	4	11	12	18
Preston	17	3	6	0	13	10	1	4	3	9	9	18
Swnsea	17	6	0	3	17	10	1	4	3	4	12	18
Wrxhm	17	5	1	2	10	5	3	0	6	9	15	17
Cardiff	17	4	2	2	9	7	2	2	5	8	16	16
Orient	17	3	3	2	13	17	1	4	4	7	10	15
Oldhm	17	4	2	3	11	9	0	4	4	6	11	14
Shrby	17	4	3	1	14	8	1	0	8	7	16	13
Wtfrd	17	4	2	2	10	7	0	3	6	3	13	13
Fulhm	17	2	2	5	9	15	3	1	4	12	16	13
Cmb U	17	2	3	3	11	9	1	3	5	8	15	12
Bris R	17	3	3	2	14	12	1	1	7	10	20	12
Chrltn	17	3	3	2	13	14	0	3	6	5	20	12
Burnly	17	1	4	4	9	12	0	3	5	11	23	9

In the run up to Christmas 1979, QPR briefly topped the league table following back-to-back home victories against Shrewsbury Town (2-1) and Charlton (4-0). After spending the last few seasons following our slow, torturous decline leading to our eventual relegation, the pull to see QPR play during this exciting period proved to be irresistible. As a result, I was part of a small group of 13-year-old schoolboys from Northampton fortunate enough to be at Loftus Road to see both matches.

Back in the late 1970s, Lings Upper School in the town's Eastern District had a number of pupils who, like me, followed the R's. During morning break on the Monday or Tuesday following the previous Saturday's draw away to Luton Town, somehow we managed to convince ourselves that it would be perfectly acceptable for us to travel down to Loftus Road to see the Super Hoops play against Shrewsbury Town. It didn't seem to matter that none of us had reached our 14th birthday, as one of the group, Paul Mackintosh, seemed confident enough he knew the way into Loftus Road.

On the morning of the match we caught the 10:30am train from Northampton's Castle Station to Euston Station. From there we picked up the London Underground Tube Train to Tottenham Court Road. The three slightly bemused 13 year olds transferred to the Central Line to our final destination, the White City Station.

Fortunately, there weren't any dramas, the three of us arrived at the ground some 2½ hours before kick-off.

Everything had gone so well, we decided to go again the following Saturday, a London derby match against Charlton Athletic.

The journey down to QPR went smoothly just as before. We knew that things weren't quite right though when it became clear that a sizeable number of Charlton fans had decided to watch the game from the QPR home stand. The stewards and police eventually cleared the opposition fans from the ground, fortunately before any trouble had started.

Sadly, after the match, in the one and only occasion that I've witnessed trouble between rival fans, the police had to push hard to calm and then regain control of the situation.

Purely by accident, our small party of 13-year-old travelling QPR fans were caught right in the middle of the skirmish. I can still remember having to jump clear of a police horse as it pushed its way through the swollen mass of supporters just outside the Springbok pub, along South Africa Road.

Worse was to follow, the police announced that they were closing the White City Tube Station to QPR fans. All home fans wishing to use the tube would have to walk down to the Shepherds Bush Station. Thanks to Paul Mackintosh, we found our way home.

Strangely, I heard that Paul swapped his allegiance from QPR to Everton shortly afterwards, something I could never understand. The day I became a QPR supporter, one thing I hadn't fully appreciated is that I'd signed up for life.

The 1970s ended with QPR languishing in the Second Division. Disappointing for the fans, although unbeknown to us all, better times were just around the corner…

In my experience, one of the strangest things about following QPR is the regular, sometimes heated discussions you'll have with your peers while travelling to see the Super Hoops play. I'm positive this isn't a situation unique to fans of QPR, although the strength of feeling doesn't get diluted by the sheer weight of numbers.

The passion felt for our club will often draw the mildest mannered of individuals into the fray. The most common cause of these highly-charged debates seems to be the subject of players, both past and present and their influence on our team.

Like lighting a fuse to a spectacular in-car firework display, the explosive cocktail of testosterone and boredom can be ignited in a second. This highly volatile mixture being slowly stirred and brought to the boil by seemingly endless congestion on our busy road network.

Even when I'm with my closest circle of travelling R's fans, people I've known for years, they often have polar opposite opinions.

At worst, there appears to be an unshakable and misguided opinion by certain individuals that below average players can become world beaters by simply donning the blue and white hooped shirt of QPR. Whereas I do believe that this probably would cause a reaction in a side made up of fanatical supporters (like me!) or in an Under 12 side, I've seen more than enough examples over the years to know this doesn't happen in professional football. Even worse, I've witnessed numerous players give significantly less than the required 100% effort when on the field of play.

I've even come to the conclusion that at least one member of the original 2015/2016 squad of QPR players doesn't actually like football. His only problem being, he obviously enjoys being paid the ridiculously inflated salary of a professional footballer.

Obviously blessed with an abundance of pace and skill but with no desire, over the last few seasons he's rarely handed his kit in after the match bathed in sweat and covered in mud; in my opinion, a pretty good indication of an individual going through the motions.

Such is the strength of opinion that very rarely will the group of QPR fans I regularly travel with get anywhere close to agreement. Certainly my opinion of Armand Traore hasn't gone down well!

Before I go on to submit my team of former QPR players in my 1970s Team of the Decade, can I suggest that if you are indeed travelling as a group, you may wish to complete the table in pencil as if your party is anywhere close to being as opinionated as ours, your initial list of players is subject to change!

I make no apologies for my opening team, it's a pretty safe one for supporters like me. Becoming a fan in 1975 and experiencing the magical 75-76 season means my opening selections for 'QPR Team of the Decade' are perhaps going to be entirely predictable.

QUIZ – 1970s

1.	What year did Dave Sexton become QPR Manager and who did he replace?	3 Points
	Your Score	
2.	How many times did Gerry Francis play for England?	3 Points
	Your Score	
3.	How many times did Gerry Francis play for England as Captain?	3 Points
	Your Score	
4.	Which club sold Dave Thomas to QPR in 1972?	1 Point
	Your Score	
5.	How many goals did Stan Bowles score for England?	3 Points
	Your Score	
6.	Which club sold Stan Bowles to QPR in 1972?	1 Point
	Your Score	
7.	Name the three clubs Stan Bowles played for (in order) after leaving QPR.	3 Points
	Your Score	
8.	Who became the QPR Manager in May of 1979?	1 Point
	Your Score	
9.	Who made his debut for QPR in April 1979 against Coventry City?	3 Points
	Your Score	
10.	What was special about the result?	3 Points
	Your Score	
	Your Final Score	

Answers on page 153

MY TEAM OF THE DECADE – 1970s

	My Selection	Your Selection
GK	Phil Parkes	
DEF	Dave Clement	
DEF	Ian Gillard	
DEF	John Hollins	
DEF	Frank McLintock	
DEF	Dave Webb	
MID	Dave Thomas	
MID	Gerry Francis	
MID	Don Masson	
FOR	Stan Bowles	
FOR	Don Givens	
SUB	Mick Leach	

A perfect blend of age, skill and experience. A team built over a number of seasons, started by Gordon Jago and completed by Dave Sexton. The team should have won the Division One league title in 1976, the fact it didn't still hurts nearly 40 years on.

CHAPTER 5

1980s

The deeply flawed relationship between the QPR owner, Jim Gregory and the team's manager, Tommy Docherty, continued into 1980. Then in early May, having just completed his first full year in charge as manager, Docherty was sacked.

Having failed to secure an instant return to the English First Division, Gregory's patience ran out. Although this proved to be a temporary parting as he'd failed to appreciate how much the manager's popularity had grown in the dressing room, he was pressurised into making an embarrassing U-turn just 9 days later.

At the time, as a 13-year-old, if I'm being honest, all I was looking for was a bit of stability at the club.

The writing was on the wall for Docherty though. Just five months later, following a sluggish start to the season where QPR had won only 3 of their first 11 games, the 'Doc' was sacked and this time there was to be no return.

In what proved to be an inspired decision, the QPR owner demonstrated his business acumen and clear understanding of the world of football; he persuaded the then Crystal Palace boss, Terry Venables, that the time was right for him to join QPR. Widely recognised within football as a gifted tactician and excellent man-manager, his appointment proved to be a real coup for QPR. Indeed, some years later Venables would go on to manage England to an 'Oh so close' Euro 1996 victory until we were knocked out of the competition by our Germanic cousins… yet again!

FINAL LEAGUE POSITIONS

1980s

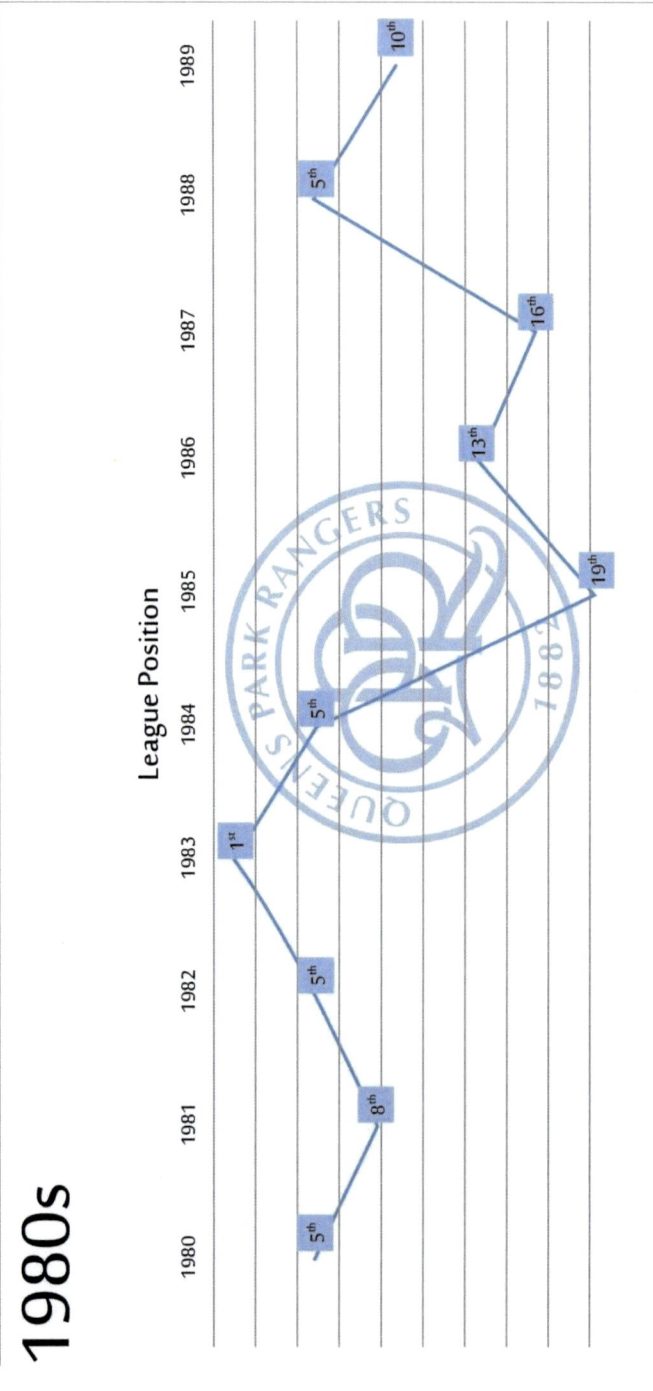

Venables was already well known to Gregory as he'd served the club so well as first team captain (as well as assisting the QPR coaching staff with player development and team tactics) some six years earlier.

Despite the rebuilding work at Palace having already started in earnest, the opportunity to work at QPR proved to be too much for the Eagles boss to ignore, most probably a simple case of Gregory's plans for QPR being a better match with Venables and his ideas for the future.

The transfer activity for the 1980-1981 season saw the talented Chris Woods (Goalkeeper) leave QPR to join Norwich City.

Players coming into the club included key personnel from Crystal Palace. Terry Venables was obviously taking the opportunity to cherry-pick from his former club's squad.

John Burridge (Goalkeeper) and Terry Fenwick (Defender) were just two of the former 'Eagles' deciding to make the short trip across London to Loftus Road.

Although he was clearly a target for Venables during this time, there was to be no swift return to Loftus Road for former QPR favourite, Clive Allen. The Super Hoops had to wait another 12 months to re-sign him from Crystal Palace.

QPR had sold Allen to Arsenal for a fee in excess of £1.2 Million in July 1980. Strangely, within a month of this high-profile signing, Arsenal sold him to Crystal Palace, with him never having played a league game for the Gunners.

In another great piece of business for QPR, Jim Gregory paid Palace a significantly reduced fee of £400k for the young striker.

Such a shrewd businessman, had he still been alive today I believe he'd shudder at the way football clubs conduct themselves, spending vast sums of money on players and salaries that are unsustainable, placing the clubs themselves at risk of financial ruin.

As well as making significant changes to their playing staff, the early 1980s saw QPR spend a significant amount of money rebuilding and modernising their home ground; Loftus Road.

The work included the installation of a second tier in the Loftus Road stand (Home fans) and School End stand (Away fans). The latter also fitting a roof for the first time!

Adding to the list of improvements, I believe that Loftus Road was one of the first stadiums in the country to have an electronic scoreboard installed.

Centrally situated, slightly above and a few meters back from the crossbar at the school end, it was often hit by wayward shots that were ballooned wide of the goal. This would occasionally cause a number of the bulbs immediately around the point of impact to fail, making the score unreadable; technology is a wonderful thing!

The most controversial development though came about in 1981 when QPR had a brand-new playing surface laid, the all-new synthetic 'plastic' pitch era had arrived.

Other teams (Luton Town, Oldham Athletic and Preston North End) would also fit fully synthetic playing surfaces, but perhaps as the first club to complete this installation, it always seems to be QPR who are associated with plastic pitches?

Now, although I count myself as an avid QPR supporter, I'm no fan of the artificial pitch. In my opinion, football is a sport to be played on grass. However, for those of us who've played Saturday afternoon and Sunday morning football, grass is a luxury that simply doesn't exist on large areas of most football pitches from October to early May. Certainly, prior to having the plastic pitch installed, it wasn't uncommon for teams visiting Loftus Road to have to play on a surface made up of 50% mud, 30% sand and only 20% grass. Not the best way to promote the pass and movement style of football that most fans admire and enjoy.

Unrecognisable from the magnificent surface of today, a few weeks into the new season the pitch at QPR could easily be confused with something being prepared for a game of beach football. Even a short period of bad weather meant that playing football at Loftus Road, before the introduction of the plastic pitch, could be challenging to say the least.

Despite my dislike of a fully synthetic pitch, given the opportunity of playing on a sand covered, semi-frozen surface or a flat and level synthetic pitch, I'd chose plastic every time. Lots of QPR fans from that time will remember the almost constant criticism the pitch attracted. Did no one ever consider that it was often singled out by the opposing manager as the difference between the two sides and the reason why his team came away from Loftus Road without any points?

I have one last observation on the subject. If you're a professional footballer, you could or should be able to play on any surface; although I do understand that regular games played on plastic can cause stress injuries. I do sympathise with players who couldn't play on such a hard surface without risking an injury, obviously footwear hadn't kept pace with plastic pitch technology. However, I do recall Stan Bowles breaking his ankle away at Bristol City when his foot got stuck in the mud when twisting to beat an opponent on a typically awful playing surface.

It must be remembered that today's superb quality pitches are made up of a mixture of synthetic and natural grass. A combination that a good groundsman and his team can work with, pretty much guaranteeing an almost bowling green finish throughout the season. This is something that skilful players of the 1970s and early 1980s could only have dreamed of.

I do find it annoying when QPR's achievements throughout the time the artificial pitch was in use at Loftus Road (1981-1988) have largely been attributed to the playing surface. It's an insult to the quality of the players and the managers at QPR during this time.

The magnificent effort of Terry Venables and his team in reaching the FA Cup Final in 1982, when we were still a Second Division club, has been undervalued because of our artificial pitch. The fact that three of the seven games played in qualifying for the final against Tottenham Hotspur were played away from home doesn't seem to matter…a case of 'why let facts get in the way of a good story?'

QPR'S ROUTE TO THE 1982 FA CUP FINAL

Round 3: Queens Park Rangers 1-1 Middlesbrough
Replay: Middlesbrough 2-3 Queens Park Rangers
Round 4: Blackpool 0–0 Queens Park Rangers
Replay: Queens Park Rangers 5–1 Blackpool
Round 5: Queens Park Rangers 3–1 Grimsby Town
Round 6: Queens Park Rangers 1–0 Crystal Palace
Semi-final: WBA 0–1 Queens Park Rangers (at Highbury)
Final: Spurs 1–1 Queens Park Rangers (Wembley)
Replay: Spurs 1–0 Queens Park Rangers (Wembley)

I pick-up the story of our 1982 FA Cup run at the Quarter Final stage; QPR v Crystal Palace.

An inevitable goal from Clive Allen secured a 1-0 home win for QPR against Palace in the last eight of the competition. In truth, the amount of chances created by QPR should have seen us through the tie by a much wider margin.

The semi-final was played at Highbury, our opponents on the day were West Bromwich Albion, a well-established First Division outfit who must have started the game as clear favourites.

Although I have watched the MOTD recording many times since, I didn't go to the match itself, instead I busied myself at home, too nervous to sit and listen to the radio.

Terry Venables was just coming up to his second anniversary of taking over as the manager at Loftus Road. Although we were still playing in the Second Division, he'd built a team that was starting to show the form and consistency needed to take the club forward.

Any team with Simon Stainrod and Clive Allen playing up front was going to score goals. With the vastly experienced Ian Gillard still playing at the heart of the QPR defence, we weren't going to concede many either.

Over the last 39 years I have learned that when it comes to football matters you usually bow to the superior knowledge of John Motson, the BBC's Match of the Day commentator. On this occasion though, I honestly think that 'Motty' got his assessment of Clive Allen's winning goal incorrect.

The whole of the QPR team played exceptionally well to beat WBA over the 90 minutes. Even on a playing surface that these days would leave a Sunday morning pub team with their heads in their hands, both defences demonstrated an abundance of skill and ability to keep the game goalless - until the 72nd minute.

A ball in from the right hand side was met by the QPR central defender, Bob Hazell. Just one of many players proving that they could not only give established teams from the top league in England a hard game, they could beat them as well.

As he broke into the WBA penalty box, Hazell had the prolific QPR striker, Clive Allen, on his shoulder. A WBA defender made a last ditch clearance, literally taking the ball off Hazell's boot as he prepared to take a shot at goal.

This is where the 20 year old Clive Allen's understanding of the game belied his years. In a fraction of a second, the QPR striker read what was about to happen. As the WBA defender struck the ball in an attempt to clear his lines, without breaking his stride, the QPR No. 9, anticipating the clearance, stuck out his right foot, meeting the ball perfectly.

The result, an unstoppable volley that flew past the opposition's goalkeeper: WBA 0-1 QPR.

I cannot agree with John Motson's match commentary at the time that the ball simply 'hit' the young striker to beat the stranded goalkeeper.

The final itself, played against one of the classiest teams in the top flight, had to be decided over two games. Again, something that's been forgotten when looking back at QPR's achievements during the early 1980s.

The disappointment of losing to Spurs in the Wembley Final was soon forgotten though as QPR played a slick and confident style of football throughout the following season's campaign.

The playing staff had changed beyond all recognition in Venables' first year in charge. By the start of the 1982-83 season, things were very different. The transfer activity at Loftus Road was very low key. The one exception was the transfer taking Ian Gillard to Aldershot soon after QPR's FA Cup Final defeat at Wembley.

Ian was the last player at Loftus Road to have played in the great QPR team of 1975-76. A true QPR legend, his transfer, after representing the R's at Wembley, was a fitting way to end his 14-year career with the club.

IAN GILLARD – QPR & ENGLAND

In the world's top leagues, as a rule, players like Gillard simply don't exist anymore. In today's never ending quest for ridiculously inflated salaries, fans of the game understand that individuals follow the career advice of their agents as opposed to 'belonging' to their club. Back in 1968 when Gillard made his debut for QPR, there was no need for players to kiss the badge on their shirts to show loyalty to the team.

As previously stated, most football fans can see when individuals aren't giving full commitment on the pitch. I suspect you'd have to sit down with Ian Gillard and try to explain the concept to him as he, along with most players from his generation, always gave their all.

Money can only ever be a short-term motivator, and whereas I fully understand the need for individuals to realise financial security, greed should not be tolerated.

Just as you start to wonder if the very worst of the winter weather will ever give in to warmer conditions, the onset of early spring seems to signal a dramatic surge for points. Certainly, in March of 1983, QPR posted an unbelievable sequence of results. The opening fixture ended with a 6-1 victory against lowly Middlesbrough. Further high scoring matches were to follow, with the R's averaging 4 goals a game in an almost unstoppable period for the Super Hoops.

The decisive manner of these victories propelled us towards promotion and probably broke the spirit of the teams behind us.

Indeed, QPR would finish the season as Division 2 Champions, some 10 points ahead of the second placed team, Wolverhampton Wanderers.

Terry Venables had built a team which had run Spurs incredibly close in an FA Cup Final in 1982; he'd now turned his attention to league matters. Promotion back to the top flight was achieved in 1983, less than 12 months after the defeat at Wembley.

The Guinness Boys, Champions of Division 2.

Unbeknown to us at the time, there was one dark cloud on the horizon; one of the most talented managers of his generation was beginning to attract unwanted attention in Europe.

After a four year absence, QPR certainly enjoyed their first season back in Division 1. Finishing the season in 5th place, with some big wins to entertain the home fans at Loftus Road (6-0 against Stoke City and 4-0 against Southampton), QPR had become a genuine First Division outfit. The mercurial talents of Terry Venables had turned a fairly average Second

Division club into a team that could compete with the recognised big hitters at the very top of the English Football League.

Sadly, in May 1984, Venables left Loftus Road. Just at a time when the situation at QPR could have turned into something really special, a mouth-watering opportunity presented itself. Venables was offered the chance to take over at the sleeping Spanish giant, Barcelona.

The Englishman was adopted by the Catalonian people. He was given the nickname 'El Tel' and proved to be an immediate success at the Nou Camp.

He signed two British strikers, Gary Lineker from Everton and Mark (Sparky) Hughes from Manchester United. Lineker proved to be a massive hit, scoring a hat-trick in his first game against Real Madrid.

In his first full season, Venables led Barcelona to the Spanish League title (their first since 1974). Perhaps most impressive of all in 1986, he took them to their first European Cup final since 1961! Only to suffer the English tradition of losing on penalties.

Filling the vacancy at Loftus Road wasn't going to be easy. QPR turned to a succession of managers, the merry-go-round continuing until Jim Smith was appointed in June 1985. His 3 ½ years in charge not only ushered in a much-needed period of stability, it also included another trip to Wembley. This time for a league Cup final against Oxford Utd.

I'm a firm believer that supporting QPR has affected my personality… unbelievably perhaps, for the better. One of many important lessons learned goes way back to that Wembley final in 1986.

QPR's route to the final included a 0-2 quarter final away victory against Chelsea at Stamford Bridge. Goals from the magnificent (and sorely missed) Alan MacDonald and Michael Robinson settled the tie.

Overcoming our West London neighbours at Stamford Bridge, would probably have been enough for many QPR fans, especially as we had been drawn against the mighty Liverpool (arguably the best team in Europe at that time) in a two-leg semi-final.

QPR went to Anfield protecting a slender lead from the home leg. An amazing performance by the R's saw us coming away from Anfield with a 2-2 draw… Surely after knocking out two of the competition's hot favourites, our name was on the cup already? Not a chance.

I hadn't yet reached my 20th birthday; following QPR for the best part of 11 years, I'd already tasted the bitterness of humbling defeats on several occasions:

Finishing second to Liverpool in the league ('75-'76), relegation from the top flight ('78), and also losing to Spurs in the FA Cup final ('82). Over the years, I'd had to come to terms with all of them. What happened next was perhaps to provide me with one of the hardest lessons of all.

It matters little who you've beaten, if you underestimate your next opponent, no matter who they are, you place yourself at a significant disadvantage.

I can now accept that we were beaten before the game had kicked-off. Too many QPR players were obviously thinking that the day was all about basking in the glory of dumping Chelsea and Liverpool out of the competition. All we had to do on the day was turn up and collect the winner's medals.

Oxford United simply pressurised us from the start, closing us down and not letting us play. By the time we realised we had a game on our hands it was already too late.

On the day, the QPR team, although full of class and quality, were, to a man, completely outplayed.

We lost the game 3-0 in a terribly one-sided affair. I'd persuaded a friend of mine, Craig Baker, [a Leeds Utd.] fan, to come to see the R's win at Wembley. The journey home was completed in almost total silence.

Jim Smith's reign at QPR would continue into December 1988 and we have much to thank him for. Under his stewardship, we regained most of the composure we lost when Terry Venables left the club to join Barcelona in 1984.

I'm not sure of the reasons why Smith left us to take over at Newcastle United. Certainly, at the time it was a difficult situation managing at St. James's Park, more of a poisoned chalice than a healthy career move.

Jim Smith's departure was a catalyst for a series of managers joining and leaving Loftus Road. On this occasion though I'm not complaining as the high turnover of managers would soon lead to Gerry Francis re-joining QPR as manager in April 1991.

QUIZ – 1980s

11.	Which sponsor followed Guinness as the brand advertised on the QPR shirt?	3 Points
	Your Score	
12.	Name the members of the Allen football dynasty that played for QPR in the 1980s	1 Point
	Your Score	
13.	Name the club that took Les Ferdinand on loan in the 1980s	3 Points
	Your Score	
14.	Which 2 clubs won promotion to Division 1 along with QPR in 1983?	1 Point
	Your Score	
15.	Name Terry Venables' long term assistant (manager)	3 Points
	Your Score	
16.	What year did the club crest change?	1 Point
	Your Score	
17.	Which club sold David Seaman to QPR?	1 Point
	Your Score	
18.	What nationality is Tony Roberts?	1 Point
	Your Score	
19.	Which club did QPR sign defender Danny Maddix from?	1 Point
	Your Score	
20.	Which club sold Mark Falco to QPR in 1987?	1 Point
	Your Score	
	Your Final Score	

Answers on page 153

MY TEAM OF THE DECADE – 1980s

	My Selection	Your Selection
GK	David Seaman	
DEF	Paul Parker	
DEF	Ian Dawes	
DEF	Bobby Hazell	
DEF	Alan MacDonald	
DEF	Danny Maddix	
MID	Gary Waddock	
MID	John Gregory	
MID	John Byrne	
FOR	Clive Allen	
FOR	Simon Stainrod	
SUB	Paul Goddard	

CHAPTER 6
A POTTED HISTORY
1990-2015

Despite the fact it doesn't appear in the title, to get a true indication of just how much has been achieved at Loftus Road, this chapter must begin way back in the mid-sixties.

In 1965, Jim Gregory, at 37 years of age, became the owner and chairman of QPR. Incredibly young to own your own football club, although this must have helped give him the sufficient drive, energy and enthusiasm to drag the club out of the doldrums, turning us into a well-established outfit within 10 years.

The meteoric rise in the club's stature almost capped at the end of the 1975-76 campaign, when our brand of 'total football' lit up the whole season. Unthinkable in today's game, QPR had seemingly come from nowhere to get within a couple of points of beating the mighty Liverpool FC to the highest domestic honour in English football.

Far from being his only contribution to the club, this proved to be just one of a long list of achievements secured by the 'Super Hoops' while under Gregory's stewardship.

QPR had already won the 1967 League Cup Final at Wembley, beating the First Division side West Bromwich Albion 3-2. The victory was made all the more impressive when you consider that we'd given them a two goal head start: not bad for a Third Division team.

Another hugely impressive fact about QPR during this time is that we were one of the few clubs to achieve successive promotions from Division 3 to Division 1. What a time to be a QPR supporter.

Perhaps Gregory's lasting legacy though is Loftus Road itself. Wedged into a tight corner of West London, he managed to turn the old ground (grass banks and all) into a stadium that most fans would recognise today. Not bad for a Fulham fan.

Indeed, it may stick in the throats of lots of QPR fans, but we do indeed have our close neighbours to thank for denying Gregory the opportunity to invest in Fulham... twice!

In addition to the huge advances being made to the infrastructure at Loftus Road, history was also being made on the field too. Gregory's connection to Fulham must have played a significant factor in us identifying the hugely talented and future Loftus Road legend Rodney Marsh. We secured his services for an unbelievable £15k in March 1966...thanks again Fulham.

I wonder just how many QPR fans realise that the long held tradition at Loftus Road of handing the No. 10 shirt to a footballing God, Rodney Marsh, Stan Bowles and to a slightly lesser degree, John Byrne, Roy Wegerle etc., started way back in 1966 and the £15k spent by Jim Gregory.

Just for the record, Marsh was sold to Manchester City in March 1972 for £200k. Later that same year, Gregory used £110k of the profit from that transfer to purchase Stan Bowles from Carlisle Utd.; again, what an inspired piece of business that proved to be.

During this period, the club's finances were never an issue, certainly never in public. How many fans like me look back with fond memories to a time when QPR made more headlines for what was being achieved on the pitch, not off it?

Whereas I'm not suggesting that Gregory was a saint, I do believe his achievements at Loftus Road have, and continue to be, overlooked and undervalued.

Certainly, the little I know regarding the details of the deal Gregory did with Marler Estates (David Bulstrode) do suggest that after such a long spell of ownership, he just wanted out.

Perhaps I'm being a little too forgiving and dismissive but as the Marler plan of merging Fulham and QPR to create Fulham Park Rangers fell through, and with the sudden passing of Bulstrode in the early autumn of 1988, perhaps it helped ease the anger over the terms of Gregory's departure.

After a single owner for 22 years, we now had our third in two years: the Thompson family.

A hugely successful (and wealthy) family, Richard Thompson was installed as Chairman at the age of 24. I can only assume that the family elders thought this was a good opportunity to see how the younger generation of Thompsons would perform when given the reins to a challenging business.

Initially, all appeared to be going well. QPR were playing some excellent football and getting some terrific results on the pitch without spending vast sums on players. It's only a guess on my part, but surely from a business perspective, the balance sheet must have been looking pretty good too?

All too quickly though, as many teams have found to their cost, failure to invest in quality players will see even the best clubs unravel.

In my opinion, football club chairmen need to have either bags of experience or a contingency plan in the event of a serious problem occurring at their club. It quickly became obvious late in 1994 we had neither. Of course we have no way of knowing how long trouble had been brewing but with the benefit of 20/20 hindsight, it's now easy to pinpoint exactly when things started to go horribly wrong at QPR: late November 1994.

After some 3½ years of being in charge, Gerry Francis left QPR following a behind the scenes bust-up, taking up the vacant manager's position at our North London rivals Tottenham.

Initially, it may have seemed that it was business as usual. Ray ('my word') Wilkins took on the managerial role at the club, and QPR would go on to finish the season in 8th place in the Premier League.

The sale of Les Ferdinand to Newcastle that summer proved to be the final straw for a QPR team now looking increasingly vulnerable to just about every other team in the Premier League.

Ray Wilkins spent the transfer money made available to him following the sale of Ferdinand on players that really couldn't begin to patch-up a team seemingly running out of energy and ideas.

Players Brought in to the Club:
- Mark Hateley
- Ned Zelic
- Simon Osbourne
- Gregory Goodridge

None of these signings could even begin to replace the hugely talented 'Sir' Les Ferdinand and the bag full of goals he scored for us every season. Indeed Mark Hateley, the player purchased by Wilkins to replace him, managed only 3 goals in his injury-jinxed career at QPR.

Sadly, and entirely predictably, we were relegated at the end of the 1995-96 season.

The Thompson family, owners of QPR since 1988, chose our relegation season as the signal that the time was right for them to sell the club.

The new owner of Queens Park Rangers FC was Chris Wright. What could possibly go wrong? A multi-millionaire and a big QPR fan, surely QPR would bounce back to the Premier League very quickly?

FINAL LEAGUE POSITIONS

1990s (relegated to Div 1)

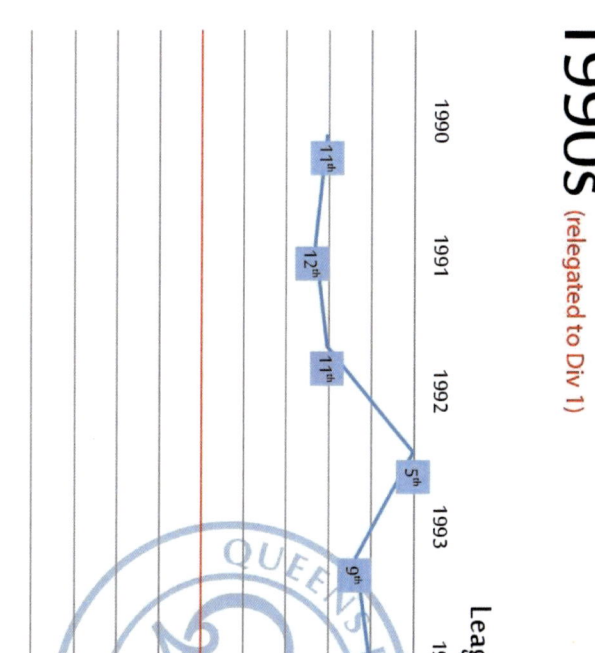

Although nobody connected with the club could have predicted the speed and ferocity of the decline in our fortunes, being relegated from the top flight of English football in 1996 proved to be a minor inconvenience when compared to some of the disasters that lay ahead in the years that followed.

Chris Wright's time as owner started with most QPR fans believing that a speedy return to the Premiership was on the cards. The reason for this optimism? For the very first time in the club's history, the new Manager appointed by Wright was effectively given a fistful of blank cheques and the only instruction appears to have been "Get us promoted." Large amounts of money were spent on players with big reputations, however none of them particularly shone in the blue and white hooped shirt.

On paper, at least, QPR had a team more than capable of gaining promotion. Certainly fans I knew weren't concerned at the amount of money being spent, our owner was a QPR fan and a multi-millionaire. If more money was needed, surely all we had to do was ask? None of this is a problem if the money doesn't have to be repaid… sadly, this is rarely the case.

Any of this sound familiar to the younger QPR fans of today? Clearly, we need to understand that investing in youngsters, even during successful periods, to maintain the squads 'freshness' is essential. Failure to do so will leave you panic buying players, leaving little or no time to ensure you get the right player(s) for the club.

Certainly, the plan to spend millions of pounds on players to gain us promotion failed and ultimately the players were sold, but at significant losses.

The debts incurred during this time would nearly force us to close. The club also had to entertain business plans from chancers looking to make themselves money out of our poor financial position; QPR merging with Wimbledon and moving to Milton Keynes was one such plan. Although this clearly worked for Wimbledon (re-inventing themselves as MK Dons), renaming and moving our club would have been too much for me.

QUIZ – 1990s

21.	Who scored the first goal in the 1-4 away win at Man Utd. 1st Jan 1992?	1 Point
	Your Score	
22.	Who did QPR sign from Saffron Walden in the late 1990s?	3 Points
	Your Score	
23.	What was the transfer fee when QPR bought Mike Sheron from Stoke City?	3 Points
	Your Score	
24.	Who replaced Stewart Houston as QPR manager in December 1997?	1 Point
	Your Score	
25.	Who bought John Spencer from QPR in May 1998?	1 Point
	Your Score	
26.	What was the transfer fee? (above)	3 Points
	Your Score	
27.	Which teams got relegated with QPR from the Premiership in 1996?	3 Points
	Your Score	
28.	Who finished as QPR's top scorer in the 1995-96 season?	1 Point
	Your Score	
29.	How many goals did he score?	3 Points
	Your Score	
30.	Who was the kit sponsor for the 1995-96 season?	1 Point
	Your Score	
	Your Final Score	

Answers on page 153

MY TEAM OF THE DECADE – 1990s

	My Selection	Your Selection
GK	David Seaman	
DEF	David Bardsley	
DEF	Danny Maddix	
DEF	Alan MacDonald	
DEF	Clive Wilson	
DEF	Paul Parker	
MID	Simon Barker	
MID	Gary Waddock	
MID	Andy Sinton	
FOR	Kevin Gallen	
FOR	Les Ferdinand	
SUB	Roy Wegerle	

FINAL LEAGUE POSITIONS

2000s

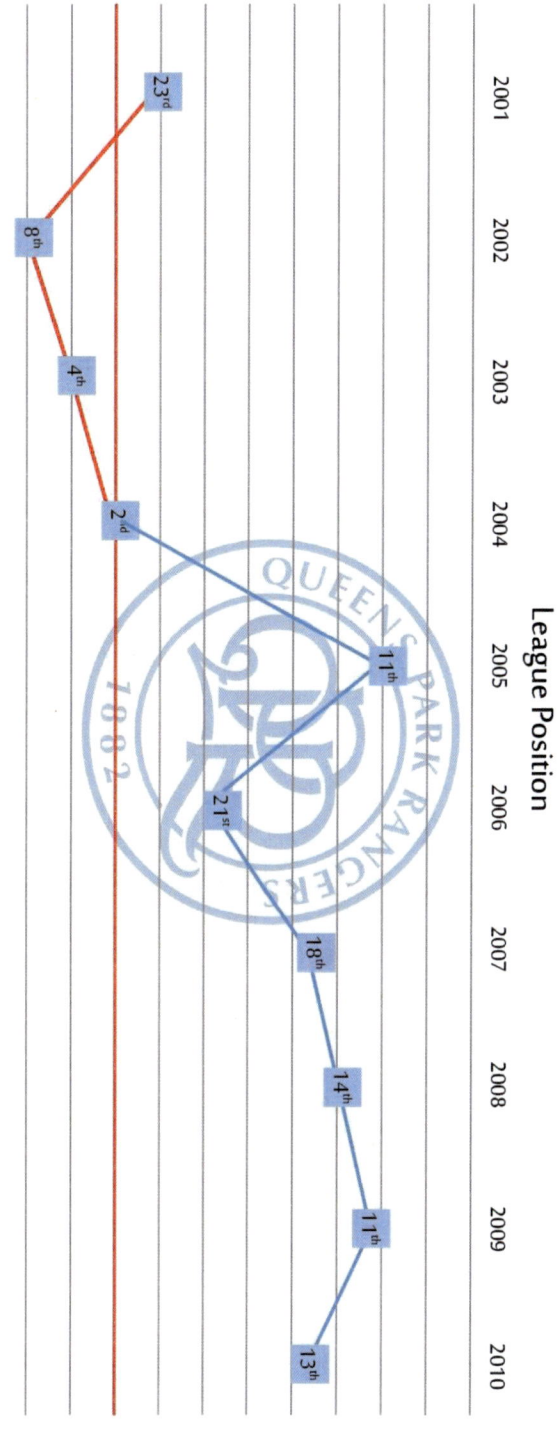

After a spell away from the club managing Tottenham, Gerry Francis returned to QPR in 1998. However, the perilous financial position of the club throughout his second spell in charge proved to be too heavy a burden for him. Despite this, he managed to guide QPR to a respectable 10th place finish in his first full season back in charge. Sadly, this was a temporary reprieve; the continued decline in the club's financial standing saw Francis resign as manager in February 2001. With Francis gone, QPR's rapid decline hit an accelerated period of free fall.

Although the hugely charismatic former QPR player Ian Holloway was appointed as manager immediately following Francis leaving the post, he could do nothing to prevent QPR suffering relegation to the third tier of English football at the end of the 2000-2001 season.

A huge debt of thanks is owed to Holloway for his stubborn, almost fanatical approach to his years at QPR, both as a player and manager. His infectious enthusiasm won over many fans doubting he had the necessary experience to manage Queens Park Rangers FC.

How wrong we were, this proved to be the perfect time and place for Holloway to demonstrate he had more than enough about him to reverse a number of the 'on the pitch' failures experienced by the club during this period. In hindsight and given the circumstances, there were perhaps very few managers around at the time who could have matched his achievements.

Season 2001-2002 – Holloway's first full season in charge - QPR slowly learned how to play with pride again. An 8th place finish was a memorable achievement when you consider the scale of changes among the playing staff at the end of the previous season.

There was of course the embarrassing defeat at the hands of Vauxhall Motors in the FA Cup, that's easily forgiven when you take a step back and look at Holloway's record at QPR. Under Holloway, we were definitely on the up!

Season 2002-2003 – The campaign proved to be another giant leap forward for the club.

Despite the appalling state of the club's finances, Holloway appeared to have the knack of unearthing quality players available for transfer at a fraction of their expected market value.

One classic example of the calibre of player unearthed by Holloway, signed initially on loan, was a 20-year-old from Watford: Lee Cook. The temporary signing saw him available to play for QPR from December 2002 to March 2003.

For such a young player, Cook's presence on the pitch was massive. I was fortunate to see him open his goal scoring account for us against a lowly Cheltenham side at Loftus Road. We went on to win the game 4-1, Cook's goal and overall contribution confirmed we'd found another gem. It was a tantalising introduction to a player with an abundance of skill and flair.

We'd have to wait until July 2004 before we'd see him join QPR on a permanent basis, however as the club struggled to find the £125k asking price.

Although QPR would go on to finish in 4th place in Holloway's second full season in charge and would qualify for the play-off final at Cardiff's Millennium Stadium (Wembley was undergoing a total rebuild at the time), we'd lose to Cardiff City in the final after a particularly 'warm' welcome from our Welsh cousins. Anyone else remember the trick with the fire alarm being set-off mysteriously in the early hours of the morning at the hotel QPR were staying in? The 1-0 defeat proved to be only a temporary setback.

Season 2003-2004 – Every club needs a catalyst, someone or something to provide the spark a team needs to move forward. From the very first day of the 2003-2004 campaign, it became obvious to most QPR fans that we'd developed into a team more than capable of doing well in the league. We were a side perhaps driven by the anguish felt by missing out on promotion back to the Championship, albeit in a play-off final a few months earlier.

On an unbelievably hot day in early August 2003 where, despite the pitch-side temperature reaching well in excess of 100 degrees Celsius, QPR totally destroyed their opening day opponents, Blackpool. The final score was QPR 5 – 0 Blackpool.

One of the goal scorers that day was Gareth Ainsworth, a summer 2003 signing from Cardiff City. What an acquisition he proved to be, a player who seemed to epitomise the blend of skill and enthusiasm running through our side.

GARETH AINSWORTH AND LEE COOK

Nicknamed 'Wild Thing', Ainsworth joined the club following our defeat in the play-off final at the Millennium Stadium. He soon became a firm favourite at Loftus Road, a superb player who could score goals from anywhere on the pitch and would run through a brick wall if QPR needed him to. An extremely brave player, he once tried to continue playing after a particularly heavy challenge had clearly left him in agony. After a few attempts to 'run-off' the injury, Ainsworth signalled to the bench that he'd have to come off, the fans warmly applauding his effort and attempts to carry on. An X-Ray would later reveal the injury to be a fractured leg!

QPR would go on to finish in second place in the league, avoiding the possibility of another 'winner takes all' play-off final lottery... for now anyway.

In July of 2004, QPR again approached Watford to check on the availability of Lee Cook. This time however, QPR managed to cobble together enough cash to buy the hugely influential player on a permanent transfer; Holloway had his man.

Season 2004-2005 – As if to demonstrate just how far QPR had come, although the signing of Lee Cook was universally welcomed by all QPR fans, unlike his first spell on loan at QPR, he'd have to earn his place on merit in a team full of quality.

Players such as Kevin Gallen, Marc Bircham, Danny Shittu, Martin Rowlands and Paul Furlong would all, of course, benefit from having Cook playing in the first team.

In total, Lee Cook scored 11 goals while playing in the blue and white hooped shirt of QPR.

A well-publicised fact about Cook is that he (and is family) are QPR fans. I'm guessing of course, but to score a diving header in front of the Loftus Road stand must have been on his 'To-Do' list ever since he learned how to kick a ball. I'm nearly 50 years old, sadly it's still on mine!

However, simply to call the goal a diving header wouldn't begin to do it justice. The build-up was a slick pattern of passing, quickly converting defence into attack. A pinpoint ball played into the penalty box from the right-hand side of the pitch found Cook. He met the cross perfectly, getting so much power on the ball, it seemed to go through the goalkeeper's hands. What made the goal so special was the way he hung in the air, the technique that comes from a natural technical ability not possessed by many football players, even at professional level.

One of the elements that made Cook an outstanding individual was his style of play, almost as if he was playing a game of football in the school playground. Refreshing to think that a modern-day footballer just loved playing for his team; money didn't appear to play any part in his motivation to play. Indeed, the incredibly difficult financial situation we were in at that time saw Cook waive the £250k due to him when we had to sell him to generate much needed revenue, our close neighbours and rivals Fulham paying £2.5 Million for his services. A true QPR legend, so short in supply over recent years.

Ian Holloway's years of managing QPR drew to a close in February 2006, almost 5 years to the day since taking charge of the club. I'm not going to dwell on the details of his departure as in my opinion it would serve no purpose. Instead, I'd like to finish this piece with a simple thank you to Ian Holloway and his time as a player and manager at QPR. He undertook an almost impossible task of keeping the club afloat when most wouldn't have come within miles of Loftus Road.

In truth, when he took over as manager of QPR way back in February 2001, he probably needed us as much as we needed him. I can't help but smile though when I look back at his years in charge, something all too uncommon with many of his subsequent replacements.

Unbelievably, it would take another 4 years and a total of 12 managers before the appointment of Neil Warnock in March 2010. Warnock's calming effect on the pitch was a real shot in the arm.

QPR QUIZ – 2000s

31.	Who played in goal for the opening fixture of the 2000-2001 season?	3 Points
	Your Score	
32.	Who did we record our first away victory against that season?	3 Points
	Your Score	
33.	What was QPR's biggest victory that season?	3 Points
	Your Score	
34.	Who was the shirt sponsor for the 2008-2009 season?	3 Points
	Your Score	
35.	Who took over as manager following Olly's departure?	1 Point
	Your Score	
36.	Who got relegated with QPR in the 2000-2001 season?	3 Points
	Your Score	
37.	Which club did we buy Akos Buzsaky from?	1 Point
	Your Score	
38.	In the play-off final at Cardiff in 2003, who should have squared the ball?	1 Point
	Your Score	
39.	How many points did we finish ahead of Cardiff City that season?	3 Points
	Your Score	
40.	Who won the league that season?	3 Points
	Your Score	
	Your Final Score	

Answers on page 154

MY TEAM OF THE DECADE - 2000s

	My Selection	Your Selection
GK	Lee Camp	
DEF	Gino Padula	
DEF	Clarke Carlisle	
DEF	Danny Shittu	
DEF	Fitz Hall	
DEF	Damien Stewart	
MID	Alejandro Faurlin	
MID	Lee Cook	
MID	Gareth Ainsworth	
FOR	Akos Buzsaky	
FOR	Adel Taarabt	
SUB	Richard Langley	

MANAGERS - FEB 2001 - JAN 2012

	Date In	*Date Out*
Neil Warnock	2nd Mar 2010	8th Jan 2012
Mick Harford	15th Jan 2010	2nd Mar 2010
Paul Hart	17th Dec 2009	15th Jan 2010
Steve Gallen	16th Dec 2009	17th Dec 2009
Jim Magilton	3rd Jun 2009	16th Dec 2009
Gareth Ainsworth	9th Apr 2009	3rd Jun 2009
Paulo Sousa	19th Nov 2008	9th Apr 2009
Gareth Ainsworth	24th Oct 2008	19th Nov 2008
Ian Dowie	14th May 2008	24th Oct 2008
Luigi De Canio	29th Oct 2007	12th May 2008
Mick Harford	1st Oct 2007	29th Oct 2007
John Gregory	20th Sep 2006	1st Oct 2007
Gary Waddock	6th Feb 2006	19th Sep 2006
Ian Holloway	26th Feb 2001	6th Feb 2006

When Warnock took over from Mick Harford on 2nd March 2010, it's fair to say QPR were struggling. Our situation was proving to be a major headache as the owners had adopted a strange philosophy where it seemed that for a while, they felt they knew more about football matters than the people managing the team. They would make some really bizarre decisions then not take responsibility when things didn't go well.

I can only assume this meddling in team affairs stopped when Warnock came along. Certainly, Warnock's reputation as a single-minded footballing man wouldn't have sat well with calls from the owner telling him to substitute player X and bring on player Y.

Warnock's appointment came at a time when QPR were perhaps at their lowest ebb, sitting in 20th position in the table, just two places above the relegation zone.

Warnock's first game in charge was against high-flying WBA at Loftus Road. A 3-1 victory eased our fears of slipping further into trouble, a sign perhaps that QPR had been underperforming for some time.

Indeed, a 20-point haul in our last 14 games that season saw us finish comfortably mid-table. A great end to the season, although I didn't hear anyone talking-up our chances of promotion the following season, especially as champions!

Season 2010-2011 – I do often wonder why it is that English managers aren't given greater opportunities at clubs in the top tier. Sadly, we appear to have promoted the myth that English managers work best with little money, working on a shoestring budget and getting the best from existing players. If big money is going to be invested, it seems that club owners prefer foreign managers.

Certainly, Warnock spent wisely in the summer of 2010. A number of key signings were made, although none of them made a sufficient ripple to attract the 'what if' brigade of pundits looking to make a story out of nothing. It seems an absurd thing to say but football sells. If you can keep the interest levels up during the summer months, then fewer people will be tempted to cancel their regular monthly payments for live football.

What a pleasure it was to be a QPR fan during this time. Warnock had built his team around Adel Taarabt, his phenomenal skill on the ball had persuaded Warnock to overlook the weaknesses in his all-round game. Warnock must have worked incredibly hard to keep Adel on the straight and narrow… it worked though. He, and QPR had a terrific time.

With the perfect blend of skill and steel, the 2010/2011 season proved to be extremely enjoyable for QPR fans. Starved of success for so long, it now seemed that we were overdosing on highly polished performances every week. Apart from the odd freak result and the possibility of us losing points due to transfer irregularities, QPR looked like champions throughout the campaign.

I have loved the successful times at Loftus Road although they are few and far between. For those of us 'in the know' there's so much more to QPR than simply winning.

I hope you enjoy *'QPR – Away Day Travels'*. Please remember it has been written by a supporter for all football fans, especially those following my club…QPR. It's not meant to be a diary, although the writing has definitely been affected by my total belief that QPR are the best club in the world, it's just that the world doesn't know that yet!

QUIZ – 2010s

41.	Who captained the 2010-11 side?	1 Point
	Your Score	
42.	Who was the leading QPR goal-scorer in the 2010-2011 season?	1 Point
	Your Score	
43.	How many games did QPR win during the 2010-2011 season?	3 Points
	Your Score	
44.	What position did QPR finish in our first season back in the Premiership?	1 Point
	Your Score	
45.	Which Man Utd player appeared to throw himself to the floor to win a penalty against us in 2012?	1 Point
	Your Score	
46.	In the 2010-2011 season, what was the QPR v Cardiff score?	1 Point
	Your Score	
47.	Who was the kit sponsor for 2010-11?	1 Point
	Your Score	
48.	In season 2011-2012, which teams got relegated from the Premiership?	1 Point
	Your Score	
49.	Which club bought Heidar Helguson from QPR?	3 Points
	Your Score	
50.	In season 2010-2011 - On the opening day who did we play, what was the score and who scored the winner?	3 Points
	Your Score	
	Your Final Score	

Answers on page 154

AWAY DAY TRAVELS

A	ARSENAL
A	ASTON VILLA
C	CAMBRIDGE UNITED
C	COVENTRY CITY
C	CRYSTAL PALACE / WIMBLEDON
D	DERBY COUNTY
E	EVERTON
L	LIVERPOOL
M	MANCHESTER CITY
M	MANCHESTER UNITED
N	NEWCASTLE UNITED
N	NORTHAMPTON TOWN
N	NORWICH CITY
N	NOTTINGHAM FOREST
W	WATFORD
W	WEMBLEY

AWAY DAY TRAVELS – A

ARSENAL FC

Nickname – The Gunners
Formed – 1886
Formed by workers at The Royal Arsenal (Woolwich)
Home Ground - The Emirates
Capacity – 60,272 (Season 2014-2015)

Quite simply the best league ground I've ever been to, a fabulous match day experience. Whereas I'm not about to turn this book into a culinary review I can strongly recommend the Chicken Balti pies for a pre-match or half-time feast. Stunning!

The stadium itself oozes class, no such thing as a restricted view here; comfortable seating and space between the rows! Not something you'd have experienced back at Loftus Road. Indeed, the chap who sits in front of me back at HQ regularly pushes himself back in his seat every time the opposition attack. I'm convinced he doesn't know he's doing it, it's a sort of nervous tick. This results in the back of his chair hitting my shins, leaving my legs looking like I've played 90 minutes of football, rather than having only watched it.

MOST MEMORABLE MATCH

ARSENAL 1 - 0 QPR
(SATURDAY 31ST DEC 2011)

By the time the two teams took to the field at the midway point of the 2011/2012 season, even the people who'd been utterly convinced that we were more than capable of finishing the season well above the Premiership relegation places were beginning to come to their senses.

The cause of the problem was QPR's self-imposed embargo on adding players to our Championship winning squad. Indeed, it wasn't until Tony Fernandes was unveiled as the new majority shareholder on 18th August 2011 that funds became available to purchase a number of new players.

Sadly, instead of what should have been a coherent plan to add to the quality of the squad following our promotion to the Premier League in the spring of 2011, a sort of panic purchase culture erupted at Loftus Road. At times, it seemed to the fans that every club had a long list of players available and waiting to join QPR.

With such a disjointed approach to strengthening the playing staff, is it any wonder that most of the signings in the six months following our promotion didn't have the skill, determination or desire of the players they had been brought in to replace? They appeared to be nothing more than a long list of Premier League journeymen, seemingly more concerned about maintaining the trappings of life as a professional footballer than putting in a performance for QPR. Added to that, the inflated wages being paid to these so-called 'stars' must have caused a great deal of resentment amongst the players who'd won the club promotion the season before.

It's a strongly held belief of mine that players who believe all the hot air blown up their backsides by agents develop an overly inflated idea of their own value. Unfortunately for the fans of QPR, we did seem to sign a disproportionate number of individuals with the wrong attitude, those perhaps who thought total commitment to the team wasn't for them and they could coast, almost as if they were there to provide the 'class' not the effort.

The number of new signings meant that instead of evolution, the fans were treated to a sort of player revolution. Somewhat surprisingly perhaps, most of us hadn't even begun to see what a mess we were getting ourselves into, although in hindsight it's now clear that we were caught up in an almost endless number of panic buys that could only ever be disastrous for the club. It would appear that no one at QPR even questioned why certain players were still available so late in the August transfer window; individuals whose only concern was perhaps in getting the right 'deal' to maximise their income, and not questioning if a move to Loftus Road was right for them, the fans and the club.

Travelling by road in London is never an exact science, so we'd given ourselves plenty of time to complete our journey to the Emirates. As a result, our small band of travelling R's arrived at this fabulous new stadium a good 90 minutes before kick-off. There were plenty of opportunities for the 3 junior R's (my son Joshua, Terry's son Ted and Lloyd's son, Matthew) to wander around the section of the ground set aside for away fans.

Having failed to attract the attention of the QPR players busily going through their pre-match warm-up routines, Joshua turned around and began to study a lone figure sitting a few rows behind us. He was instantly recognisable as Anton Ferdinand, the QPR central defender recently signed from Sunderland, not playing on the day due to injury.

I can only guess that Ferdinand was trying to disguise himself, simply wanting to watch the game from the stands in amongst the travelling fans. He obviously couldn't have done a good job; with an 8-year-old boy blowing his cover in seconds! In truth, Mr Ferdinand looked every bit the stereotypical footballer. Indeed, his baseball cap and dark glasses probably cost as much as most family cars at the time.

I do sometimes wonder if there's a recognised list of 'must haves' for professional footballers immediately after signing professional contracts with league clubs. If that is indeed the case, there's probably a personal shopper hovering outside the owner's offices at most football grounds when the two annual transfer windows open, just waiting to assist the players, helping them look the part and spend their newly found wealth "wisely".

Taking that a stage further, do the manufacturers of prestige cars have representatives available 24/7 throughout the months of January and August? Again, if that's the case, is there a standard protocol with certain marques available to Premiership players (Aston Martin, Bentley and Ferrari) through to League 2 professional footballers with a more modest income, perhaps attracting interest from more mainstream manufacturers?

This isn't meant to come across as a criticism, it's just an observation on possibilities open to the high earners in British football. Such is the kudos of being involved with a Premier League football club, you get the impression that even the tea lady drives a brand-new Porsche at clubs who regularly finish in the top half of the table.

There is however one point that, in my opinion, needs to be addressed, this being the apparent inability of some footballers not to render their vehicles near worthless by ordering pointless and in some cases ridiculous additional options. A bit like a going for a curry with friends who request too many side orders, even though everyone sitting around the table knows that they will only spoil the main dish.

Perhaps professional footballers should be forced to stick to standard options for things like paintwork finish, wheels and interior colour choices. As an example, I'm pretty sure whoever it is in London's West End that I've seen driving about in a black Bentley with a matt paint finish is either a lottery winning nightclub doorman or a professional footballer!

QPR's visit to the Emirates on New Year's Eve 2011 is the only time I've ever been to the hugely impressive new stadium. Perhaps, somewhat predictably, in the middle of a difficult campaign, QPR lost the match, albeit by a single goal after gifting Robin Van Persie a simple opportunity to score on 60 minutes.

It's so frustrating to see QPR work so hard to produce some intelligent and entertaining football only to switch off for a second and concede a goal. Of course what didn't help matters was the error made by the match officials shortly before Arsenal scored. A goal kick was awarded when clearly the ball had rolled out of play having last touched an Arsenal player.

The resulting clearance up field saw QPR quickly regain possession, only for Shaun-Wright Phillips to lose the initiative cheaply with a misplaced pass to Arsenal's Tomas Rosicky. The Czech Gunner immediately played a defence-splitting pass through to the in-form Robin Van Persie. His clinical strike from 12 yards out cost us all 3 points.

Ultimately, the result mattered little, as in a season full of momentary lapses of concentration that would cost us so many points, we'd avoid relegation by the smallest of margins.

QPR fans (and football fans in general) are a very resourceful bunch, unearthing humour where perhaps you'd least expect it.

Certainly on the day, the mood amongst the away supporters was a little tense, until that is, everyone visiting the Emirates was treated to a song sung by the QPR fans to the tune of 'The Lion Sleeps Tonight',

"Queens Park Rangers, the mighty Rangers, we never win away". "We never win away, win away, oh win away, win away, we never win away".

Following our defeat at the Emirates, QPR would start 2012 in 17th position, just 2 points from the third relegation spot.

Sadly, for me, one of the things highlighted in recent times is that I most definitely carry a grudge. It doesn't seem to matter if events influencing my dislike of a team or player in some instances could have occurred many years ago, I just can't seem to let them go.

It's difficult to put my finger on exactly why I developed such a dislike of Arsenal FC, although I can tell you it lasted for the best part of 20 years. Probably the result of several events: the David Seaman transfer, being locked-in for what seemed like ages after the game had finished and being marched around the old Highbury Stadium like naughty schoolboys before being allowed to find our way home, possibly even their negative style of play.

Top of the list, of course, had to be the protracted David Seaman transfer. Easily the best goalkeeper in the league at that time, his desperate desire to leave Loftus Road came as an insult to those of us would have gladly paid to play for our beloved team.

I fully understand footballers are not always driven by money and, in hindsight Seaman did indeed have an eye on winning silverware, his subsequent transfer to Arsenal gaining him several top honours which would have remained out of reach had he stayed at Loftus Road.

What didn't help was the delay in the transfer being finalised, this after the QPR keeper had been photographed smiling and shaking hands with representatives from the North London club, even wearing an Arsenal shirt! A little premature as the delay saw Seaman available and picked to play for QPR again before the season drew to a close.

As you can probably imagine the whole episode didn't sit well with the QPR fans. To his credit though, the QPR keeper kept his pre-match routine exactly the same, although somewhat predictably for those of us in the ground early enough to witness it, what happened before the start of the game immediately following the delayed transfer will live long in the memory.

In the days before football stadium terracing was replaced by row upon row of seating, a QPR fan (and his girlfriend) had taken up position just behind and to the left of the goal in the Loftus Road stand. This chap, obviously incensed with the poor handling of David Seaman's imminent transfer, took it upon himself to let the 'want-away' keeper know exactly how upset he was. There he stood for an age, shouting and hollering a stream of expletives at the QPR goalkeeper.

At first it was funny, however, the more the crowd laughed and jeered at the abusive fan, the worse he got, with his girlfriend looking deeply embarrassed, trying to calm him down without success.

Throughout the tirade, David Seaman remained pokerfaced; a true professional, he just continued with his pre-match routine. The QPR coach, Roger Cross, fired shots at the goalkeeper, one to the left then one to the right, all the time while coming under what had now become a venomous attack from the disgruntled fan. His girlfriend was tugging at his jacket, desperate for him to stop the abuse; she was now close to tears.

The poor chap really had lost the plot, it seemed that getting no reaction from David Seaman was actually making him worse. He needed something to bring him back to his senses, and whilst I'm not sure if was through design or misfortune, that's exactly what happened!

With perfect comedy timing the supporter's girlfriend pulled one last time at his jacket, he turned his head continuing his verbal onslaught just as Roger Cross unleashed a perfect half volley that sailed past the post.

The verbal assassin didn't see the missile coming, the ball hit him squarely on the cheek bringing instant silence. Silence quickly turned to laughter all around as our dazed fan visibly wobbled on his feet, David Seaman even allowed himself a chuckle before continuing with his warm-up.

Did Roger Cross aim his shot at the abusive fan? You'd have to ask him that!

My overriding memory of the Arsenal team from the late 1980s to the mid-1990s is seeing Tony Adams with his arm in the air claiming an offside against a poor member of the opposition who'd sadly fallen asleep while watching the Gunners attempt to fashion a shot on goal. Typically, so boring was the 90 minutes of the actual game, I'm pretty sure most Arsenal fans wanting to see a few shots on goal went home after the pre-match warm-up... all that changed in 1991 with the signing of the hugely talented and prolific goal scorer, Ian Wright, from Crystal Palace.

HISTORICAL INFORMATION

Early in 1990, QPR secured a 2-0 victory in the Second Round of the FA Cup against Cardiff City. Although the draw was yet to be made, I somehow knew that we'd meet Arsenal in the next round, as somewhat predictably they won their own 2nd round match 0-1, away at Stoke City.

My worst fears were soon realised when QPR were indeed drawn to play against Arsenal at Highbury.

ARSENAL 0 - 0 QPR
(SATURDAY 27TH JANUARY 1990)

Perhaps, somewhat predictably, the game itself finished in a drab 0-0 draw; like watching a game of chess, only without the punch and excitement!

The highlight of the afternoon was when the QPR fans standing immediately in front of us, obviously a little worse for wear, started singing derogatory songs about the Arsenal substitute Perry Groves with as much gusto as if they were the backbone of a Welsh Choir singing at a Royal Wedding. For reasons of taste, I won't include the songs sung about the former Arsenal skipper Tony Adams as it became common knowledge shortly after the game that he had a drink problem.

QPR 2 - 0 ARSENAL
(WEDNESDAY 31ST JANUARY 1990)

Unlike the stale, boring match at Highbury a few days earlier, the replay a few days later was a classic. A vintage performance from a rampant Rangers side saw us romp home 2-0 with goals from former Arsenal favourite Kenny Sansom and the superb Andy Sinton.

Sansom's goal, an accurate shot that found the bottom corner of the net after a number of despairing attempts to clear the ball, had left the Arsenal Goalkeeper unsighted.

In truth, the goal forced the Gunners to break with tradition and make a game of it. Had our North London opponents scored first they would simply have defended for the remainder of the game, effectively killing the match as a contest. In my opinion, it was a travesty that so many quality players in an Arsenal side capable of doing so much more were restricted to playing a dull, unimaginative style of football.

The second QPR goal settled the tie. Andy Sinton's effort was a carbon copy of many goals he scored over the years he played in the blue and white hooped shirt of Queens Park Rangers.

Often, from a central position, Sinton would drag the ball over to the left hand side of the pitch before cutting back onto the right. Once inside the opposition's penalty box he'd hammer a shot past the hapless goalkeeper.

It was a truly memorable night (and result) that will live long in the memory of those of us who were there to witness it.

AWAY DAY TRAVELS – A
ASTON VILLA FC

Nickname – The Villains
Formed – 1874
Home Ground - Villa Park
Capacity – 42,682

MOST MEMORABLE MATCH

ASTON VILLA 0 - 1 QPR
(WEDNESDAY 24TH SEPTEMBER 2008)

The preliminary rounds of the annual League Cup competition start pretty much as the new league campaign begins in August. All 72 football league clubs play in the first round of the competition with most of the Premier League clubs joining in the second round.

Yet again, you don't have to dig too deeply to find a member of the so-called elite of English football acting in a disparaging way or making misguided remarks about the value of winning this domestic cup competition. In 2010, Arsene Wenger is quoted as saying that "Winning the League Cup won't end Arsenal's trophy drought." Surely, even the manager of Arsenal cannot fail to understand the damage he has done? The English game has 92 league clubs, all of which have a responsibility to their fans to try to win every game they play. It is important to remember at this point that Arsenal belong to that group and that the group doesn't belong to Arsenal. By publicly admitting his team has little interest in winning the League Cup he undermines and undervalues the trophy.

Arsenal are a big club, one instantly recognisable to football fans across the world. Surely though they understand their responsibility to the fans of English football? Not just those choosing to follow Arsenal, all fans within this country. I suspect that the Arsenal Manager has his eye on the bigger, more lucrative cup competitions involving teams from Europe... please be careful Mr Wenger!

My 'Most Memorable Match' begins with a short reference to an identical fixture, almost 4 years before.

On the 22nd September 2004, Terry Cadby, Lee Edmonds and I travelled to Villa Park to see our newly promoted Championship side take on Aston Villa of the Premier League. I can't remember exactly why, but I was nominated to drive, but my little Ford Fiesta lacked the pace and power to get 3 fully-grown men to Birmingham quickly and in any sort of comfort. Having to keep the engine spinning quickly to get anywhere close to the speed limit, especially in the stop-start traffic of Birmingham's nightmare motorway network known as 'Spaghetti Junction', meant I had to go through the gears like a seasoned Formula 1 driver.

To avoid embarrassing the individual concerned I won't name the person who felt it necessary to talk me though every gear change, every overtaking manoeuvre or even when to apply the brakes. Although, I will say that out of the 3 of us in the car, Terry was preoccupied trying to remember the name and location of a 'terrific' curry house he'd been to in Birmingham some weeks before and I was driving!

We parked the car in what can only be described as a piece of grassed wasteland, all bumpy and uneven. I can't believe that if it was indeed derelict land, why it hadn't been purchased and houses built on it?

I'm not complaining though, the 'car park' was completely fenced in and had an attendant wandering around, £5 well spent for peace of mind! Unlike my first visit to Villa Park back in 1992, where TC had driven Lee Edmonds and me to the game in his bright red XR3i. The car was hugely popular with thieves; indeed, you might have thought that one of the optional extras offered by Ford when buying the car from new was a fully trained guard to sit in or close to the vehicle while you were away.

Having parked his 'thief magnet' in one of the many side streets located close to the ground, a small group of youths had gathered around the vehicle even before the engine had been switched off. They all wanted money to 'look after' TC's car, in typical Terry fashion he instantly invited them to "P**s off". In case you're wondering, the car was fine.

The 2004 cup match saw QPR put in a plucky performance against David O'Leary's side. Although Villa would go on to win the tie 3-1, it turned into a lesson in how to take your chances as opposed to being totally overwhelmed and outclassed. QPR could, and really should, have made much more of a game of it, the Super Hoops striker Paul Furlong failed to convert two straightforward opportunities with the score at 2-1.

As can often be the case with football, just when QPR had built up a head of steam and were looking the more likely to score, they were hit by a sucker punch.

We pushed forward in search of the equaliser, our defence becoming more and more stretched as the tempo of the game increased. A cheaply conceded free kick deep inside the QPR half gave Nolberto Solano an opportunity to launch an unstoppable shot beyond the despairing dive of our goalkeeper. The ball sailed into the net, putting the tie out of QPR's reach.

FINAL SCORE: ASTON VILLA 3 - 1 QPR

At the start of the 2008-2009 season, QPR would again be drawn away against Aston Villa at the same stage of the League Cup competition.

Queens Park Rangers could now be considered as a reasonably well-established Championship side. Up to this point we'd never dallied too close to the top or bottom of the league for prolonged periods, more often than not looking every inch like a mid-table side.

However, this repeat fixture did give us an opportunity to assess just how far as a club QPR had come in the four years since we'd last met.

In truth, the almost endless managerial merry-go-round experienced at Loftus Road since our last meeting meant that any comparisons drawn from this game would be shallow and inconclusive at best. With rumours of the owners picking the team and the manager, Ian Dowie, little more than a 'yes' man to them, perhaps understandably things would quickly start to go backwards.

On the night though, all of that was forgotten. If I'm being honest, we were more than a little bit lucky to come away from Villa Park with a victory. Our game plan appeared to be to defend deep and hit them on the break or from a set piece... and, amazingly it worked.

That evening proved to be one of those rare occasions in life where everything works in your favour.

1. A VICTORY FOR THE SUPER HOOPS

For QPR to win away against Premier League opposition was uncommon last season (2014-2015) when we actually played in the top flight. Way back in 2008 when we were a championship team obviously the opportunity to play against the cream of English football was extremely limited. Therefore, a victory against Aston Villa was one to be savoured. We rode our luck and came away from Villa Park with a 0-1 victory against a tough, combative Villa side managed by Martin O'Neill.

2. LIFE WITH THE 'PRAWN SANDWICH' BRIGADE

In my first taste of luxury at an away fixture, I was fortunate enough to receive the last two tickets for a fabulously appointed executive box for helping my wife with hosting duties before, during and after the game. I'm certainly not complaining, a three-course meal, Guinness and a lift there and back made for a really enjoyable evening. Although, I have to say I missed the sense of belonging you get from being in amongst your own fans. The second ticket? That went to Terry Cadby as Mr Edmonds was busy doing other things.

3. I BACKED THE FIRST (AND ONLY) GOALSCORER

I'm usually rubbish at betting, as if to highlight just how bad I am, this is the first and only time I've called and backed the first goal scorer.

It wasn't that inspired a decision though, as QPR were most likely to score from a set piece; with our big central defender, Damien Stewart, often getting on the end of a corner. His sheer size and strength often caused havoc in the opposition's penalty box, and so it proved to be. Stewart scored from a corner, I think it was the 78th minute. QPR hung on for a much-needed morale-lifting victory.

A superb victory, watched from an executive box and going home with more money in my wallet at the end of the evening than when I started. If only there were more nights like these!

Back to earth with a bump in the next round though. Another fixture against Premiership opponents, this time Old Trafford and a small pub team called Manchester United.

We'd lose the game 1-0, a match where it was obvious from the start that we had no intention of trying to win, we just wanted to avoid being heavily beaten.

Much more of a problem for us though was losing the services of Akos Buzsaky. He suffered a serious cruciate knee ligament injury, which kept him out of the team for months.

QPR had lost a player at a crucial time in the season and without him, the QPR side, all of a sudden, looked pedestrian at best.

HISTORICAL INFORMATION

The first and most obvious recollection I have for QPR v Aston Villa matches will resonate with many fans of a certain vintage. The date, 22nd February 1977, the match, the 2nd leg of that season's League Cup competition.

The final score of Aston Villa 3 – 0 QPR was marked by a stunning performance by Brian Little, sadly something not mirrored by his personality. An understated man with an abundance of flair and ability, but with a grey and inverted personality, his skills on the pitch were not fully appreciated as his dull and colourless nature failed to lift the public's perception of this truly gifted individual.

Villa would eventually go on to win the League Cup in 1977, thanks to the goal scoring achievements of Brian Little. I believe that thanks to him they were destined to win the competition from the very first round. Such was Little's impact that season, his name, not that of Aston Villa, should have been engraved on the cup. Everything Little did in front of goal seemed to end up in the back of the net, as QPR found to their cost.

Again, somewhat unbelievably, at a time when the English game was starved of genuinely talented individuals, Little made very few appearances for the national team.

At the time of writing, the last match I attended at Villa Park dates back to a bitterly cold night early in 2012.

QPR were once again fighting against the very real prospect of relegation back to the championship less than 6 months after a return to the top flight.

We'd raced into a two goal lead, only to be pegged back by a Villa side also struggling with the prospect of a bottom three finish.

FINAL SCORE: ASTON VILLA 2 - 2 QPR

Oddly enough, it's not the match itself that I want to include in Away Day Travels. It's my attempt to record the kind and caring attitude of your immediate circle of friends when you spill your hot food or drink.

Before we took to our seats in the stand, Terry, Lee and I queued for a hot drink and a pasty from the refreshments counter, nothing unusual there as we always grab at least a drink before kick-off.

We walked the short distance to our seats carrying our hot food and drink, without incident, the rapidly cooling food steaming in the freezing conditions.

As a seasoned follower of football over many years, I'd never dream of going to a football match at that time of year without wearing layer upon layer of clothing to keep the chill of the night away. Unfortunately, on this occasion the layers of clothing served only to compound the problem.

What I'd failed to notice is that the lid to my coffee cup hadn't been fitted properly. As I tried to take the first warming sip of the hot beverage, nothing happened.

Although it took only seconds for me to realise what was happening, I was soaked. The hot liquid had just found its way through the layers of clothing on to my skin... ouch! The cooling night air had reduced the scorching heat to an uncomfortable burning sensation by the time the steaming brew had reached my jeans.

What it did mean though was my lap had received a good soaking. To the untrained eye, it looked as if I'd failed to reach the toilet in time to empty my bladder! To add insult to injury, the rapidly cooling 'wet patch' was now beginning to cool in the freezing ambient temperature. I was in for a long night.

Added to the visual and obvious physical discomfort I was experiencing, there was the embarrassment factor to deal with. Terry, never one to let an opportunity for a wind-up to pass him by, was busily telling as many people as he could that I had wet myself. The dark, completely sodden area on my jeans added support to his story... charming!

As for Lee, he was wearing one of those pained expressions where he desperately wanted to be sympathetic but was clearly fighting with his conscience. An occasional grin and even a chuckle was escaping from my less than concerned friend.

Just for the record, had the spillage occurred to anyone else, somewhat predictably, I'd have laughed my socks off. Indeed, way back in 2003, when Lee and I had travelled down to Loftus Road to see QPR play in the third tier of English football, there was a classic example of ball vs. tea cup prior to kick-off.

In a thousand to one shot, just as a supporter was heading for his seat with his steaming beverage, a player took a shot at the QPR goalkeeper. The wayward effort missed the goal by a significant margin, the gentleman carefully carrying his hot drink obviously hadn't realised that he'd just entered the 'kill-zone' so was blissfully unaware of the missile heading towards him.

The ball scored a direct hit. Hot tea exploded everywhere, with the polystyrene cup disintegrating on impact. In my defence, my first reaction was to check that no one had been hurt… sadly, this was quickly followed by my second: laughing!

AWAY DAY TRAVELS – C
CAMBRIDGE UTD. FC

Nickname – The U's
Formed - 1902
Home Ground - Abbey Stadium
Capacity – 8,127

MOST MEMORABLE MATCH

CAMBRIDGE UTD. 1 - 4 QPR
(SATURDAY 20TH NOVEMBER 1982)

Throughout the 1981-82 season, QPR were already beginning to show flashes of the skill and determination needed to mount a serious bid for promotion. Indeed, as if to underline the team's growing capability, QPR would go on to reach the FA Cup Final in the spring of 1982 (only to fall at the final hurdle, losing to Spurs in a tightly contested replay).

Following such fine performances and with Terry Venables at the helm, QPR would indeed go on to become Second Division Champions in 1983.

Known today as the Championship, it was one of the first pieces of silverware brought back to Loftus Road since the 3-2 victory in the League Cup Final against WBA in 1967.

Under Venables, QPR added consistency to their performances; it's almost as if you could see the players' self-belief growing with every game.

A player who flourished during this time was the young QPR striker, Clive Allen. Indeed, the two very different goals he scored in the 1 – 4 away victory against Cambridge United demonstrated a player at the very top of his game.

His first strike was an example to all youngsters interested in football of the importance of being able to dribble the ball with both feet. Allen ran in from the left hand side of the pitch towards the Cambridge United goal, preventing the ball from going out for a goal kick with his left foot. Without taking another touch, he simply rolled the ball past the hapless goalkeeper from what looked like an impossibly tight angle with his right boot.

QPR fans hadn't seen such a gifted out-and-out striker since the glory days of the ridiculously underrated Rangers legend: Don Givens.

At a time when world-class players in the English game were at a premium, Allen's second goal was something special, easily a contender for the goal of the season in the English leagues (probably throughout Europe too). Had the goal been scored by Bergkamp, Di Canio or Suarez then it would have been shown repeatedly in recognition of what can be achieved with a football. Sadly though, when a goal of real class is scored by an Englishman, especially one playing for a club from the second tier, it's almost as if it doesn't count!

Like all top strikers, Allen had the gift of finding space for himself when it mattered most, enabling him to score a simple tap-in, or as on this occasion, to convert an unbelievable effort.

A fine ball played into our host's penalty box was knocked down for Allen by his striking partner, Simon Stainrod. At this point you wouldn't have thought that Cambridge were about to concede their 4th goal of the afternoon. Until that is, Allen, with his back to the goal and the ball at his feet, calmly scooped the ball over his shoulder. The instantaneous 180-degree switch in the direction of play completely wrong footed the opposition's defence. The Cambridge players could only watch as the QPR No. 9 smashed the ball beyond the goalkeeper. A timely reminder that as well as possessing the instincts of a natural goal scorer, he also had an abundance of great flair and skill.

In an absolute footballing travesty, Clive Allen would only represent England on 5 occasions.

HISTORICAL INFORMATION

CAMBRIDGE UTD. 2 - 1 QPR (SATURDAY 29TH SEPTEMBER 2001)

Ian Holloway had taken over as QPR's manager in late February 2001, although he could do little to prevent our slide into the Second Division a few weeks later.

During the summer of 2001, following our relegation to Division 2, Holloway presided over a monumental shake-up of the playing staff at Loftus Road. No fewer than 16 players left the club, a mixture of individuals no longer wanted or their wages proving to be unaffordable for a club playing in the third tier of English football. Perhaps the only exception to this was the sale of an extremely valuable and lucrative asset: Peter Crouch.

A final 'gift' to the club from Gerry Francis, he'd bought the youngster from Spurs for just £60k in July of 2000. QPR sold him to Portsmouth for £1.5 million 12 months later.

Even with this substantial windfall, the financial situation at the club remained perilous. With the crippling level of debt incurred by the Super Hoops over recent seasons, only 6 players came into the club before the 2001-02 season got under way.

When you consider that the majority of the first team players had only known each other for a few weeks prior to the start of the new campaign, it soon became clear that Holloway had done a superb job of rebuilding QPR with very little time and money to complete the exercise.

Although the season had started well for us, we were still learning how to play against some of the division's more 'physical' teams. Therefore, a 2-1 defeat away at the Abbey Stadium on the 29th September, 2001 wasn't completely unexpected.

The difference between the two clubs on the day proved to be their up-and-coming striker; Dave Kitson. Very much in the mould of an 'old fashioned' centre forward, Kitson battered and bruised the QPR defence into submission.

On the whole it was a nasty and aggressive fixture, a classic example of a team playing to their strengths. QPR lost 2-1 in the autumn gloom gathering around the Abbey Stadium. This was going to be a long season!

If I'd purchased my ticket and had been sitting in the away stand in amongst the travelling QPR fans that day, I'd most definitely be shouting and screaming at the referee to get control of the game. Not today though, I had to be strictly 'neutral', as I went to the game as a guest of one the match officials, Richard Beeby.

It's an odd feeling to be at a football ground on a Saturday afternoon and not be able to express yourself.

It reminded me a little of my early years at school as the summer holidays approached; a time when even the most responsible and dedicated of students could get swept away by the excitable atmosphere. Until that is, you were taken to the year above for an introduction to their world. A strange, almost surreal experience where you were in amongst familiar faces, although somehow you knew that you were expected to act in a calmer, more adult-like manner.

I've always thought Richard was a good referee, although in the interests of impartiality I've decided to let my fellow R's supporters speak for me.

I have been able to find a refereeing league table on the editor Clive Whittingham's excellent network 'Loft For Words', an absolute must for all QPR fans. It lists Richard's ratings from match reports from QPR fixtures going back to the 2005-06 season.

The table shows him climbing from 17th position, rising to 4th before slipping back to 6th place in his final season before retiring at the end of the 2008-09 campaign.

Whereas I'm not about to disagree with any of the reports or subsequent scores given to Richard following his performances at Loftus Road, I must point out that from what I understand, it certainly doesn't appear to be easy to get the right number of 'ticks in-the-boxes' to progress as a match official without stifling a great deal of common sense. The fact that he finished his time as a referee in 6th position in the referee's league table means that he was able to find a pretty good balance between executing the laws of the game and keeping fans happy.

I was fortunate enough to attend a number of matches with Richard over a period of a couple of years or so, including going to Loftus Road on a couple of occasions. Although I very much enjoyed the experience of going 'behind the scenes' at QPR, for me, the best part of the day was walking out on the hallowed Loftus Road pitch.

A few weeks before the away defeat at Cambridge Utd., Richard offered Terry Cadby and me tickets for the QPR v Birmingham City pre-season friendly. A low-key affair compared to league fixtures, we were even allowed on to the pitch to 'inspect' the playing surface; it was immaculate.

Well before the ground was opened to the R's fans, I took the opportunity to wander around the pitch. Savouring every moment, I slowly walked out to the right-hand side of the goal in front of the Loft.

I picked the moment that, had I been able to smuggle a ball onto the pitch, I would have launched it into the top corner of the net.

Indeed, I'd have been so desperate to score a goal for the Super Hoops in front of the Loft, if someone was recording the goal attempts I'd finish the season with the highest number of attempts recorded for the season (even if I only played for 45 minutes!) Come on you R'ssssssss.

AWAY DAY TRAVELS – C

COVENTRY CITY FC

Nickname – Sky Blues
Formed – 1883 (Singers FC)
Home Ground - Ricoh Stadium
Capacity – 32,609

MOST MEMORABLE MATCH

COVENTRY CITY 0 - 1 QPR
(WEDNESDAY 26TH AUGUST 1992)

How times have changed! Of the 22 players starting this league fixture (QPR's 4th match of the inaugural Premier League season), only the QPR Goalkeeper, Jan Stejskal was born outside of the United Kingdom.

Coventry City	*QPR*
Steve Ogrizovic	Jan Stejskal
Peter Atherton	David Bardsley
Kenny Sansom	Alan McDonald
Andy Pearce	Darren Peacock
Lee Hurst	Clive Wilson
Stewart Robson	Andy Sinton
Micky Gynn	Ray Wilkins
David Smith	Simon Barker
Terry Fleming	Andy Impey
John Williams	Dennis Bailey
Robert Rosario	Les Ferdinand

A startling statistic, when compared to our Premier League fixture of 12th April 2015, where only 11 of the total 22 players starting the match were British. Somewhat unbelievably, 9 of those players were from QPR! Although I'm sure everyone connected to English football will tell you our Premiership is the best, most competitive league in the world, the facts also seem to suggest our home-grown footballing talent isn't the reason behind this. Most successful Premier League clubs regularly start their matches with very few (if any!) players born in England. Is it just a coincidence that our national team has been going backwards since the introduction of the Premier League, with the excessive number of foreign players in just about every team?

It's a problem that cannot be ignored as the pool of English, world-class talented youngsters appears to be shrinking. There appears to be a very real possibility that, left unchecked, the number of overseas players plying their trade in our leagues will, given time, severely weaken the English national team. This could, over time, result in us becoming uncompetitive and lucky to qualify for the World and European tournament finals in years to come. If further evidence is needed, just look at Scotland's rapid demise in the world of international football in recent years.

Perhaps I should just keep following England's fortunes as they promise lots but deliver little. At the time of writing, a world ranking of 9th perhaps should be celebrated and accepted as a worthwhile achievement in itself. The trouble is, in truth I'm desperate for us to win something, to beat the best in the world at the game that has dominated my life since I became overwhelmed by its magic as a 9 year-old boy.

As a youngster, the frustration of seeing England fail on numerous occasions would often lead to me voicing my concerns during a match, something my parents simply couldn't understand.

On one particularly memorable occasion I must have had steam coming out of my ears, in an attempt to avoid the usual response from my parents of "Grow up Simon" I decided to try to pre-empt the inevitable 'telling off' by explaining exactly why I was so annoyed.

The match was Scotland v England, broadcast live from Scotland's Hamden Park stadium. The reason for my outburst? Ray Clemence, the usually highly dependable England goalkeeper had just let the ball creep through his legs and roll almost apologetically into the back of the net. My parent's response? "I'm sure he did his best." Unbelievable!

Being a devout QPR fan, I've never knowingly passed up an opportunity to go and see them play, even when returning early from my honeymoon with my wife of 4 days due to the appalling weather experienced on the south coast.

After driving over 300 miles back from St. Ives, I then jumped back into my little 1100cc Ford Fiesta and drove up to Coventry to see QPR play. Having arrived back in Northampton too late to join up with or even contact the regular 'QPR - Away Day Travellers', they had no idea I'd be joining them at the game. I caught up with Terry, Lee and Lloyd on the open terracing set aside for the away supporters just before kick-off. Once the jokes and chatter had died down we settled into the game.

It's only perhaps when you look back at the 11 players starting this fixture that you begin to appreciate the quality we had running through the side. Certainly, that night QPR took all 3 points back to Loftus Road after a clinical strike from the underrated Andy Impey.

Rangers took the lead just as the first half was coming to a close. A ball played up to Les Ferdinand from Alan MacDonald was laid back directly into the path of the young Rangers starlet, who smashed the ball into the net for his first ever Premiership goal.

The QPR manager at the time, Gerry Francis, having taken over from Don Howe some 14 months earlier, had drilled the need for consistency into the entire squad. We were capable of beating anyone in the league in the 1992-1993 season, often securing victories against more fashionable teams, especially at Loftus Road. Tottenham, Nottingham Forest and Everton (home and away) were simply being thumped, conceding 4 or 5 goals to scintillating QPR performances.

Impey's strike and overall performance saw us secure a much-deserved win. I know the season was only 4 matches old, but the 3 points picked up at Highfield Road took our tally to 10 from our first 4 games; enough to put us on top of the Premiership table. Indeed, QPR would finish the season as London's top club in 5th place.

HISTORICAL INFORMATION

COVENTRY CITY 4 - 1 QPR
(SATURDAY 19TH NOVEMBER 1977)

It was a cold, bleak day, the sort that froze the end of your toes and fingers the second you left the house. Still, the prospect of going to your first away match with Terry Cadby and Lee Edmonds as well as a busload of other schoolmates took the edge off the mid-morning chill.

Living in Northampton's brand new Eastern District, a new town sitting on the outskirts of the old one was just the best. Indeed, my allegiance to QPR must have been severely influenced by living amongst the first generation of families moving up to Northampton from West London.

Coventry City v QPR, not a fixture that would get the pulses racing for many neutrals, although I can't remember many spare places left on the bus that day.

All these years later it still remains the strangest way I've ever travelled to a football match; in a 'hop on, hop off' bright red, London (Routemaster) bus. Not that there were any takers for jumping on or off our specially commissioned bus that day. It's not as if we were going to break any speed limits, with a maximum speed of no more than 50mph we were more of a rolling roadblock, never daring to, or completely unable to venture out of the nearside lane.

When being offered the chance to go and see QPR play, none of the 50 or so pupils who'd decided that it was a good idea had even considered that the reason for leaving school at 11am was down to the mode of transport.

It's not that we were expecting a brand-new coach, fully air-conditioned, with a bar and refreshments being served all the way there and all the way back. It is true to say however, we also hadn't expected to travel in an open-backed, double decker bus in mid-winter!

The day didn't get any better when the match-day tickets were handed out either. Have you ever known a Coventry City fan? No, me neither, so when we discovered we were to be sitting in the home end, my heart sank. I'm not complaining, but as a school teacher booking 50 or so tickets for a Division 1 match in 1977 with a school full of youngsters who 99.9% of them had moved from London within the last 2 years, why on earth would you purchase tickets in the home stand?

With my blue silk scarf with bold white lettering clearly identifying me as a 'Q. P. Rangers' supporter, I decided to remove it from my wrist and tuck it inside the collar of my jacket. I won't name any names, but one of the kids travelling that day had written 'QPR Are Magic' and 'Qeens Park Rangers FC' on the back of his jacket in black pen! Obviously spelt incorrectly, although I have to say when you've just arrived at the opposition's ground, having sat in a double decker bus for the last 2 hours, you'll find that your embarrassment threshold has risen significantly!

Unlike my first visit to Loftus Road where QPR had beaten WBA 1-0, my first away day ended with a sound thrashing. QPR were hammered 4-1 by a mediocre Coventry side. The only thing that made me laugh back then and still makes me chuckle today is Terry Cadby missed the only QPR goal scored by Don Givens. He was in the queue for a meat pie! An early example of TC demonstrating his overwhelming love of food!

In truth, he'd missed little in the way of entertainment, Don Givens scored a scrappy goal, no more than a token consolation from 90 minutes of rubbish. Not that we missed the opportunity to tell Terry that we'd just witnessed an early contender for the 'Goal of the Season.'

Just for the record, I have been to the new home of Coventry City FC, the Ricoh Stadium, on a couple of occasions. The ground is easy to get to, car parking isn't a problem and the ground offers the home team all the benefits of a new facility. However, this turn-key solution comes at a price, namely the cost to the club for 'renting' the stadium from the owners.

Sadly, the club appears to have fallen into a cycle of decline as a direct result of the costs associated with playing their home games at a new stadium. Something we, as QPR fans, will have to consider when a move away from Loftus Road is on the cards.

AWAY DAY TRAVELS – C

CRYSTAL PALACE & WIMBLEDON FC

Nickname – Glaziers or Eagles
Formed - 1905
Home Ground - Selhurst Park
Capacity – 26,255

This may sound a little odd but my first and only visit to Selhurst Park on the 15th February 1997 wasn't to see Crystal Palace at all; our hosts that day were their ground sharing partners, originally from Plough Lane, Wimbledon FC.

At the time, Selhurst Park was a ground that even as a QPR fan I can say was a 'classic', a throwback to a bygone era, when clearly money was tight and people (and even football clubs!) had to spend their limited resources wisely, often patching-up and repairing something that really needed replacing.

The stands were old, the wooden seating belonged in a museum and the pitch was dry, hard and had huge grass free areas. In short, the game was never going to be a classic.

Clearly my visit was a long time ago and I'm sure things have improved significantly since. Although I have no intention of going back any time soon to check. Not that that's an immediate concern as at the time of writing Palace are a Premiership team and we are not!

WIMBLEDON 2 - 1 QPR
(SATURDAY 15TH FEBRUARY 1997)
FA CUP 5TH ROUND

Our starting line-up for the 5th round of the 1997 FA Cup was as follows:

Goalkeeper	Jurgen Sommer
Defender	Alan McDonald
Defender	Steve Yates
Defender	Karl Ready
Defender	Rufus Brevett
Midfielder	Paul Murray
Midfielder	Simon Barker
Midfielder	Trevor Sinclair
Midfielder	Gavin Peacock
Forward	Mark Hateley
Forward	John Spencer

A good team that could, perhaps even should have overcome the physical and direct style of play so favoured by Wimbledon during that time. Indeed, it was this tactic that saw Wimbledon FC cause the biggest FA Cup Final shock in generations at the majestic old Wembley stadium way back in 1988, overcoming Liverpool FC 1-0.

As if to underline their hard-line approach to the 'beautiful game' an early challenge on a Liverpool player by the tough tackling Vinnie Jones was followed by him allegedly saying to the opponent, still writhing in agony on the floor, "I'm going to rip your ears off and spit in the holes" … charming!

A flurry of goals in a 15-minute spell either side of half-time saw QPR take the lead on 41 minutes through the former England international striker, Mark Hateley. Sadly, Wimbledon quickly hit back, equalising on 44 minutes and then taking the lead on 55 minutes. Goals from Marcus Gayle and Robbie Earle proved too much for us, the game finishing 2-1 to our hosts.

MOST MEMORABLE MATCH

QPR 6 - 0 CRYSTAL PALACE (SUNDAY 9TH MAY 1999)

A battered and bruised QPR squad approached this final match of the 1998-1999 season with a home fixture against our South London rivals: Crystal Palace. A string of poor results in a bad season for QPR had left us needing a win from this final fixture to avoid the drop into Division 2 (the third tier of English football).

Largely the result of poor financial decisions in trying to get us back to the Premiership, we'd been left with crippling debts and a playing staff who just didn't appear to care (sound familiar?)

As the sun shone down on Loftus Road that day, the QPR players put in an equally sunny performance, beating Palace 6-0. In truth, most of the goals were efforts born out of sheer endeavour and a gritty determination to win at any cost, something akin to a Sunday morning cup tie in one of the many leagues to be found across the country. The pick of the goals came from Tony Scully, the Rangers' winger (and former Palace player) thumping a volley into the net from a position wide on the right hand side of the pitch.

A great goal that helped keep us in the second tier of English football, albeit not for long. After a brief respite from our regular battle against relegation, we'd finally succumb to the chronic debts and an aging squad of players. QPR were relegated at the end of the 2000-2001 season.

AWAY DAY TRAVELS – D

DERBY COUNTY FC

Nickname – The Rams
Formed - 1884
Home Ground- Pride Park, Derby
Capacity – 33,500

MOST MEMORABLE MATCH

DERBY COUNTY 2 - 4 QPR
(SATURDAY 24TH OCTOBER 2009)

A fantastic run of results stretching from 29th August to this superb victory at Pride Park on the 24th October saw the Super Hoops claw their way up from 14th position in the league to the very edge of the play-off places. Early days I know, but following a three match winning sequence that saw us score 4 goals in each of the matches played, QPR fans, starved of success for so long, had started to believe that, at last, we had secured a foundation to build on.

Up to and including the victory over Derby, QPR's league record was as follows:

| P 9 | W 6 | D 2 | L 1 | GD +13 | PTS 20 |

However, those of us who'd started to think that QPR were on our way back up the Championship table, or even perhaps on the verge of having a team capable of challenging for promotion to the Premiership, were about to come back to earth with a mighty bump.

Our record following the Derby game:

| P 33 | W 8 | D 10 | L 15 | GD -19 | PTS 34 |

Indeed, less than 2 months after the free-flowing away victory at Pride Park, the QPR Manager (Jim Magilton) was sacked for allegedly fighting with one of his players! Whereas I'm pretty sure that aggression is part of daily life at other football clubs, only QPR would see fit to go on and make public the behind the scenes failures at the club.

Not that there was any visible sign of discontent amongst the QPR team that late afternoon in October.

A lively opening to the first half saw Derby County take the lead after just 10 minutes, Paul Dickov firing past the QPR Goalkeeper Radek Cerny.

Further misery was to follow for the R's after our central defender, Damien Stewart, was harshly judged to have committed a foul in a dangerous position on the edge of the penalty box. A well struck Robbie Savage free-kick saw QPR go 2-0 down after 36 minutes.

Over the last 40 years, I have developed a dislike (for one reason or another) for most teams in England. Not Derby though, until that is, they signed Robbie Savage. I simply can't stand the fella; anyone who's played for Manchester United during their hugely successful period under Alex Ferguson must have a reasonable level of ability. Savage though appeared to have settled for being a more combative player on leaving Old Trafford. I've not studied the player in great detail, indeed, my opinion of him is mostly based on what I've seen of him on TV as I can't recall him being a 'stand-out' player whenever he visited Loftus Road.

I struggle to understand why some players who make it through to becoming professional footballers appear to thrive on being labelled as dirty or aggressive. Even more unbelievable is how can they be allowed to create careers as match pundits after their playing careers are over. Surely, to glamorise thuggish behaviour sets a bad example to youngsters playing football at any level?

I know that football is a contact sport, but having watched the recent friendly between Italy and England in Turin (31st March 2015), what the hell was the German referee doing when Harry Kane was being consistently mugged by the Italian defenders?

In years gone by, great teams have had their tough tackling individuals to help play against 'lesser' opposition who try and spoil football games by intimidating skilful teams. In my opinion, the match officials need to up their game as they have all of the powers necessary to control these thugs.

It took Derby County less than 40 first half minutes to go 2 goals to the good, much to my dismay, with Savage scoring Derby's second. Despite QPR having plenty of the game, it was looking increasingly like QPR could be on the wrong end of a heavy defeat.

Not today though, as the QPR team was packed with skill, pace, power and determination. In a blistering seven-minute spell of play spanning the end of the first half and the start of the second, QPR scored two quick goals to wipe out the deficit.

The first was from Adel Taarabt, a free kick that bent and curled past the Derby defensive wall, skidding beyond the despairing dive of the Derby goalkeeper into the bottom corner of the net. The second was a well-worked move with Taarabt taunting and teasing the opposition's defence, sending over an inch perfect cross to the back post. Wayne Routledge met the ball, intelligently heading it down into the path of the onrushing Gavin Mahon to score: Derby 2-2 QPR.

It was a strange atmosphere, even at 2-0 down, you could sense that the QPR fans packed into Pride Park knew the game was far from lost.

The army of travelling fans had helped turn the game on its head, constant QPR pressure saw the R's create many opportunities, with Derby offering little in return.

Looking back at some of the members of the team that day, it's perhaps easy to understand why individually and collectively QPR gave Derby such a torrid time.

MIDFIELDER - AKOS BUZSAKY

A player who oozed class and ability, regularly proving too much for teams in the Championship to handle. On his own, he was able to provide a cutting edge to any team and when given the opportunity to team up with the rest of the QPR midfield that day, he became simply irresistible. There can be little doubt that Buzsaky was more than capable of playing at a higher level.

MIDFIELDER - ADEL TAARABT

Simply the best player to wear a hooped shirt for generations. Not since the days of Marsh and Bowles had QPR fans seen a player as talented as Taarabt. A handful on the night, the Derby players were given a kind of sneaky preview of what was to mesmerise just about every team the following season (2010-11).

MIDFIELDER - ALEJANDRO FAURLIN

Faurlin proved to be a player who has simply become better and better in his time at QPR. The type of professional who could convince anyone he could play football as he makes the game look ridiculously easy. Has the knack of playing a short or long pass with perfect timing and accuracy.

Sadly, at the time of writing he's still recovering from a second serious knee injury. All too often an unsung member of the team, I suspect that lots of QPR fans are hoping that next season (2015-16), he'll be able to return to his role in midfield for a prolonged spell without further injury concerns.

MIDFIELDER - GAVIN MAHON

A hugely influential player in his short time at QPR; a no nonsense midfielder who offered protection to the Super Hoops' defence. His goal in this game also proved that he could get forward and score in a more attacking midfield role.

MIDFIELDER - WAYNE ROUTLEDGE

The combined level of skill, pace and power offered by Routledge made him an incredibly effective and exciting player in his time at Loftus Road, something we've not truly been able to replace.

I can't quite put my finger on the reason why, but I always had the feeling Routledge wasn't a happy man while he wore the blue and white hooped shirt. Indeed, I remember the day he was introduced to the QPR fans having recently signed for us. To me the expression on his face was a simple "What the heck am I doing here?"

With further goals from Jay Simpson and Akos Buzsaky completing the amazing victory, QPR recovered from being 2-0 down to secure a 2-4 victory.

A simply magical experience that as a fan you witness on very few occasions. Certainly the journey back to Northampton after the game flew by as we each took it in turn to recount our match highlights.

Fortunately, the journey from Northampton to Derby is a relatively short one as we had a car full that day. Terry Cadby (43) his son, Teddy Cadby (11), his father, Dave Cadby (68) joining my son Joshua (6) and I (43) …the reason for listing the members of the party and their ages at the time will become apparent shortly.

QPR fans, like football fans in general are great company and often find reasons to laugh when frankly there is little to laugh about.

I was diagnosed with Parkinson's disease way back in May 2003. The battle against this degenerative condition is a tough one, often leaving me feeling exhausted and in need of regular periods of rest. I'm the first to admit that the effort needed to counter the symptoms of the disease have left me looking older than my years, although I wasn't quite ready for the conversation that took place during the away fixture at Derby.

A QPR fan walking on crutches came and sat next to me, and although it didn't bother me, he obviously didn't like to sit in silence. Having decided he was going to strike up a conversation, he leant forward, took one look at our party of five, looked at me and asked "Are these all your children?" Cheeky b*****d!

I've always enjoyed my trips to see QPR play away at Derby's Pride Park, although as with any new stadium there is always a degree of characterless repetitiveness. Despite this, Pride Park seems to have an almost timeless charm, usually associated with older football grounds. A great atmosphere and a fantastic day out.

AWAY DAY TRAVELS – E

EVERTON FC

Nickname – The Toffees
Formed - 1878
Home Ground - Goodison Park
Capacity – 39,573

MOST MEMORABLE MATCH

EVERTON 0 - 1 QPR
(SATURDAY 20TH AUGUST 2011)

Given the circumstances (having just been promoted back to the Premiership and losing our first game so heavily just seven days before this fixture (QPR 0 – 4 Bolton)), what a fantastic result for the R's. A truly classic example of QPR's ability to make my whole weekend a great one with a performance and victory that even at this early stage of the season gave us all hope for the future.

A battling performance saw QPR dominate long passages of play against an Everton side demonstrating they have enough flair, skill and determination to beat the best the Premiership had to offer.

To come away from such a tricky fixture with 3 points certainly lifted the spirits of the travelling fans, and our belief in our team's ability to survive in the big league was restored…for another week at least!

QPR took the lead on 31 minutes after a period of passing and movement that saw the Everton defence struggle to contain a Rangers side bristling with creativity. Any team possessing the individual talents of players such as Adel Taarabt and Akos Buzsaky will create opportunities. The fact that QPR started the match with both of these footballing greats in the team from the off meant our hosts were in for a treat!

Sadly, as a club we failed to learn the valuable lesson of the day; the victory was achieved by the players who had won promotion the previous season. What was needed was enhancement, not wholesale replacement.

The journey up to Liverpool proved to be a good one, back in 2011 I had a Vauxhall Zafira (seven seats) so the six members of our exclusive QPR away day travel club were all in the same vehicle. It may sound a little daft but with the three amigos and our sons travelling together, the atmosphere had started to build well before we'd made it to the M1.

Having the boys with us adds another dimension to the journey, obviously the in-car discussions are always tailored to suit the younger R's. We all have to give our score predictions, the boys will often run through the names and the qualities of some of the opposition's players. With the six of us taking our turn to enlighten the rest of the Away Day club, perhaps somewhat predictably this part of the journey swallows a large part of the overall travelling time.

Due to his wildly exaggerated margins of expected QPR victories, by far and away the most optimistic QPR fan I've ever known is Terry's son, Teddy.

I've already stated that my near 40 years of following Queens Park Rangers has made me a hopeless optimist, however Ted is without doubt a QPR basket case. He is an academically gifted lad, although when it comes to QPR he clearly suffers from a massive 'blind-spot'. In truth, I wish I could be as much of a believer as he is. To give you a classic example, he honestly believed that at 5-0 down against Manchester City recently, QPR could stage a comeback to end all comebacks. If only - we'd go on to lose the match 6-0! This confirmed our relegation from the Premier League.

The remaining journey up to Liverpool was punctuated by several stops at motorway service stations liberally scattered along the way. Toilet breaks, more food, visits to the shop, even letting the youngsters run off some of the excitable energy built up in the car by playing football all add extra time to your journey. None of this is a problem though as we always allow more than enough time for breaks in the driving.

In all of the years we've travelled up and down the country I cannot recall ever missing the start of a QPR match; home or away. Having said that, I did miss the entire first half of the QPR match on the 23rd August 2003 against AFC Bournemouth. Although when you consider that I'd been carrying out the duties of being the Best Man at the wedding of Lee and Paula Edmonds until well after midnight the day before; I think I should claim that one as null and void!

Certainly for the away match against Everton back in 2011, we arrived in plenty of time for a walk around the ground. Goodison Park is a great 'old school' football ground, situated in amongst back-to-back terraced housing making it a true focal point for the local community. You can almost taste the history of the place, the success and failures over countless seasons locked within its walls. Is it any wonder though, when you think about some of the quality players who've worn the Everton colours over the years? Dixie Dean, the bustling, free-flowing Englishman who scored a bag full of goals in his time at the club. Alan Ball, a fully paid up member of the victorious England World Cup winning team of 1966, Gary Lineker and of course the former QPR legend, Dave Thomas, whose transfer to Everton in August 1977 left me in tears.

The Everton fans seem to have an incredibly balanced view of football. Shortly before we entered the ground, we stood and chatted as Terry had gone to get us all a programme. As a group of away fans it has honestly never occurred to us to hide our team colours or even think about telling our sons not to wear any one of their QPR shirts to a fixture. The reason for outlining this? Obviously having easily identified us as QPR fans, a staunch Evertonian, wearing his Blue shirt, scarf and hat stopped by our small group and shook everyone's hand. He took the time to wish us all well and welcomed us back to the top tier of English football. It's not so much that we thought there would be any trouble from the home fans, but we most definitely weren't expecting such a warm welcome to Goodison Park.

Once inside the ground, our seats gave us a perfect view of the pitch. Indeed, the build-up play leading to our goal took place immediately in front of us. A treat for the younger members of the party as it's not uncommon for them to have to watch the game peering over the shoulder of a fidgeting adult, bouncing out of his seat every time we press forward.

I can honestly say that my one and only visit (so far) to Goodison Park has left me with a lot of great memories. It's not just the result as there's so much more to an away day than that. The classic stadium with its vibrant atmosphere, the warmth of our hosts towards us and enjoying the fun and laughter had while travelling up to the game.

After the match we made our way back to the car. The queue to exit the car park was a long one, so another member of our group (Terry Cadby), obviously still feeling the 'buzz' only a QPR victory can bring, grabbed the football off the back seat and told the boys to look and learn by watching the master.

Terry's intention had been to launch the ball into the early evening sky, then to the amazement of the youngsters, he'd instantly bring the ball under control just before it hit the ground. In reality, he hoofed the ball high into the heavens, with the ball veering so far off to the right even a fully charged 100-metre Olympic record holder wouldn't have got to it.

The ball, when it landed, scored a direct hit on the roof of a car parked close by; master indeed! Luckily for Terry, the ball hadn't damaged the vehicle, the biggest dent had been in the boys' belief in Terry's footballing ability.

HISTORICAL INFORMATION

Over the years QPR v Everton fixtures have proved to be high octane affairs. Indeed, if you start with our 5-0 demolition of the Toffees way back on October 11th 1975 (Francis 2, Givens, Masson, Thomas), we've played Everton on 41 occasions. Those fixtures have generated 123 goals; an average of 3 goals a game.

It's not just the amount of goals, in the 1990s, two highly entertaining matches saw Les Ferdinand and Bradley Allen chalk-up back to back hat-tricks for QPR.

Home or away, the clashes between these two clubs have thoroughly captivated and entertained the fans. Sadly, with our relegation back to the Championship at the end of the 2014-2015 campaign, we'll have to miss the passion and drama this fixture has brought to us by the bucket load in years gone by. I can only hope we won't have to wait too long to play the Toffees again.

AWAY DAY TRAVELS – L

LIVERPOOL FC

Nickname – The Reds
Formed - 1892
Home Ground - Anfield
Capacity – 45,276

When I visited Anfield for the first time in 2011, I couldn't help but feel a little let down by the place. To see the venue which had intimidated many of the world's best football teams over the years looking a little dated and decidedly 'ordinary' was incredibly disappointing. I guess in my mind, having visited a number of the top stadiums in England during the 2011/2012 season, I was in some way expecting Anfield to be the best of the lot. It was almost as if I'd expected the magical atmosphere created by so many crucial European and domestic victories over the years to have somehow soaked into the concrete and steelwork structure of the old stadium, leaving the visiting fans feeling anxious and concerned from the kick-off; it didn't.

Yes, QPR would go on to lose the match, but in a season full of missed opportunities, our 1-0 loss to Liverpool proved to be yet another example of a team coughing and spluttering their way through 90 minutes of football. We could have, moreover we should have, left this fortress of English football throughout the 1970s and 1980s with a point.

From memory, a glaring miss from the less than prolific Shaun Wright-Phillips ensured we were sent home without a point.

MOST MEMORABLE MATCH

LIVERPOOL 1 - 3 QPR
(SATURDAY 30TH MARCH 1991)

I'll start this section by stating just for the record that I have nothing but respect for the Liverpool team I grew up with in the 1970s, 1980s and early 1990s. Their almost total domination of domestic and European football highlighted the quality that ran through their team. With the creative genius of Kenny Dalglish, the prolific finishing of Ian Rush and the sublime skills of John Barnes and Peter Beardsley (to name but a few), at anywhere near to their best, the Anfield reds were simply unstoppable.

I do however have one criticism, a frustratingly regular occurrence of the strange phenomenon, known universally as the 'Anfield Penalty'.

Often a gift to Liverpool FC from the match officials, it is used to great effect to overcome resilient performances by teams up and down the top tier of English football. Indeed, perhaps unsurprisingly to most, a little research on the subject identified Liverpool as the side awarded the most penalties since the Premier League was formed.

1st	Liverpool	119
2nd	Arsenal	117
3rd	Manchester United	111

I'm joking of course, but the conspiracy theorists amongst us could probably build a good case of wrongdoing. The often bizarre and bewildering decisions given at Anfield by the match officials certainly give the impression that they were being guided by a set of rules that nobody else was aware of.

It certainly looks to me that most referees officiating at Anfield must, without thought or consideration, give a penalty for any of the following:

<u>1.</u> A Liverpool player is on his backside in the penalty box
<u>2.</u> The Anfield crowd shout 'Penalty'
<u>3.</u> A Liverpool player falls to the ground under a challenge anywhere on the pitch but still manages to make it into the opposition's penalty box before finally coming to rest

Is it possible that perhaps in years gone by, Liverpool awarded every referee visiting the Anfield club for the first time with a pristine LFC shirt? Signed by the home team players with a No. 12 printed on the back in recognition of the continued support of the match official. However, failure to implement any one of these directives could result in them being asked to return the shirt, instantly removing their traditional bragging rights to be known as the Scousers' 12th man!

Indeed, as if to prove the existence of the 'Anfield Penalty' syndrome, in an interesting statistic, from the five league matches that QPR played at Anfield from 1986-87 to our first away victory in the 1990-91 campaign, Liverpool were awarded three penalties. Not a bad average at 0.6 spot kicks per game!

1986 – 1987	Liverpool 2 – 1 QPR
1987 – 1988	Liverpool 4 – 0 QPR (Penalty)
1988 – 1989	Liverpool 2 – 0 QPR
1989 - 1990	Liverpool 2 – 1 QPR (Penalty)
1990 – 1991	Liverpool 1 – 3 QPR (Penalty)

Way back in 1991, a superb performance from a lively and vibrant QPR team saw us secure a richly deserved victory, our very first over Liverpool at Anfield.

A fully charged Les Ferdinand opened the scoring early in the first half with a diving header, throwing himself at a ball crossed in from the left from the excellent Simon Barker.

On a dull overcast afternoon QPR continued to press, and their constant pressure and high-energy football was rewarded when Roy Wegerle pounced on a stray back-pass from a Liverpool defence looking increasingly out of sorts. The QPR No. 10 took the opportunity to round the stranded Liverpool goalkeeper and score from an acute angle.

At 0-2, there proved to be no way back for our hosts, even the obligatory and highly dubious 'Anfield Penalty' wasn't enough to save Liverpool from defeat.

The third goal came from a simple tap-in from the superb Clive Wilson after the Reds again, uncharacteristically, failed to clear the ball from deep inside their own penalty box.

In truth, the days of the mighty Liverpool teams of the last three decades were well and truly in decline. Yes, there have been a number of cup victories, including a stunning victory in 2005 where a truly magnificent comeback in the Champions League saw Liverpool recover from a 3-0 half-time deficit to beat AC Milan on penalties.

The last 24 years have seen Liverpool fail to secure a single league title, whereas the new 'juggernaut' of English football has been the Scousers' deadly rivals, Manchester United.

The Red Devils' roll of honour during the same period includes an almost unbelievable number of major successes at home and abroad (13 league titles and 2 European Champions League victories).

The comparative lack of success at Anfield over generations of Liverpool fans has led to another phenomenon unique to the club; the 'Suicidal Scouser'.

It can't be easy for the followers of a once formidable team such as Liverpool, used to winning silverware season after season, being beaten by another English club, especially when that club happens to be Manchester United. What I find hard to understand though is the amount of Liverpool fans contacting the BBC Radio football show after the games have been completed on a Saturday evening, who cannot see their once great team is far from being guaranteed a top four finish in the Premier League…welcome to the real world!

I believe Liverpool will come good again, I'm confident there's a league title with their name on it not too many seasons away. However, I cannot see any future Liverpool side getting anywhere close to emulating the successes of the 1970s and 1980s. A classic case of a proud club with an almost unbelievable tradition of success not being able to lay that ghost to rest.

Beating them at their own ground in their heyday, albeit just the once, proved to be one of the sweetest victories ever, certainly for me.

HISTORICAL INFORMATION

QPR 3 - 2 LIVERPOOL
(WEDNESDAY 21ST MARCH 2012)

In May of 2012, QPR managed to avoid an instant return to the Championship by the smallest of margins. This midweek fixture against Liverpool at Loftus Road proved to be one of the highlights of a campaign drawing to a close with a sequence of tense dogfights.

Don't get me wrong, any victory is something to be savoured, especially when your team desperately needs points to avoid relegation. The sad truth is though, our first season back in the Premiership for some 15 years proved to be a huge disappointment for anyone and everyone connected with QPR.

The majority of all football fans, certainly the ones I've known over the years, will always expect their team to put in a performance, regardless if they're winning or losing.

Sadly, all too often that season the QPR players left the field after a full 90 minutes of play looking far from being a spent force. There's no hiding the truth on a football field, fans know when players haven't tried. Even more frustrating for the supporters is the look of a player who simply doesn't care.

The QPR team of March 2012 was a shadow of the side that had taken the Championship by storm only a few months earlier, key changes to the starting eleven had most definitely taken their toll. As a result, the opening exchanges looked as if Liverpool were more than capable of taking the victory and the 3 points home with them. Such was their dominance at times it looked as though they were able to carve out opportunities to score at will.

Finally, QPR buckled under the pressure. In the 53rd minute the sad, sick feeling you get when your team concedes a goal you feel certain will cost you the match finally arrived. An almost comical piece of defending saw the ball ping pong around in the QPR penalty box before Liverpool's Seb Coates put us all out of our misery with an acrobatic scissor-kick, the ball flew beyond the despairing dive of the QPR goalkeeper.

An equally bizarre piece of defending cost us another goal in the 72nd minute. This time Dirk Kuyt scoring from close range as QPR again repeatedly failed to clear the ball.

With 18 minutes left to play, surely it was just a matter of watching Liverpool run down the clock playing 'keep-ball', frustrating the QPR players and supporters alike.

Not today though, in what seemed like a mixture of desperation, determination and finally some self-belief, QPR simply refused to stick to the script. Liverpool played their part of course, a classic example of a team finding that once you've switched off, it's not always possible to switch back on again.

Shaun Derry started the amazing turn around, a goal scored with an unbelievable leap and equally amazing header. The stakes were so high that my first reaction was to check that the match officials had given the goal. Clearly being a QPR fan of nearly 40 years has left its mark! Some 10 years or so before I'd seen a very similar situation where the goal had been disallowed; the match QPR v Crewe, a game we had to win to keep the possibility of gaining an automatic promotion spot alive.

Our chances of beating Crewe that day were severely dented when Clarke Carlisle scored a perfectly good goal, only to see it chalked-off by a poor referee making the first of two incorrect, match-changing decisions. To add insult to injury, Carlisle was booked for what I can only assume was for viciously heading the ball into the back of the net!

Carlisle was sent-off shortly afterwards for a second bookable offence. This time a quick-thinking member of the opposition kicked the ball at the retreating QPR player, only for the referee to interpret that he'd deliberately blocked the pass after conceding a free kick. Footballers know when a referee is a plonker, so in my opinion the player knew he'd have a chance of getting Carlisle sent off if he kicked the ball at him.

Had the match official taken the time to think about his decision, I'm confident he would have waved 'play on' because had the ball missed the defender it would have gone directly to a QPR player. At the risk of repeating myself, I believe referees have a difficult job to do. What I find difficult to understand is they seem to want to make the task even harder for themselves?

Loftus Road is a great place to be when QPR have their tails up, not that we have to be winning, just simply when the players are obviously 'up' for the challenge.

Despite the fact that we had less than 20 minutes to go, after we'd scored our first goal the evening took on a completely different feel. From being timid and lacking direction, the players seemed to rekindle the team spirit and passion that had won us promotion less than 12 months before.

The equaliser, when it came, was somewhat poetically scored by the former Liverpool striker Cisse. A fine finish from a player with an abundance of skill and the ability to be in the right place at the right time.

With the end of the match no more than seconds away, it seemed that both teams would finish the game with a share of the spoils. In truth, our lowly league position and poor points tally meant we really needed a victory to give us the 3 points to keep our hopes of staying in the Premiership a realistic possibility.

QPR continued to push, probing the Liverpool defence for any sign of weakness. In a final throw of the dice, QPR had brought on another striker, Jamie Mackie and his ability to run at the opposition with the ball proved to be exactly what was needed.

In the 2 years since arriving from Plymouth Argyle, Mackie had quickly become a firm favourite with most QPR fans. His 'never-say-die' approach to playing football proved to be a breath of fresh air. Certainly, the energy and enthusiasm he brought onto the field that evening did enough to win us the game.

In typical fashion, running in towards the Liverpool goal from the right hand side of the pitch, Mackie did enough to hold off the tired challenges of a number of Liverpool players before calmly sliding the ball underneath the advancing goalkeeper.

The crowd went wild as the ball ran towards the unguarded net, almost willing the ball over the line. The QPR players had under performed for the majority of the match, all that was forgotten in an instant! Mackie simply stood with his arms open wide, a statement aimed at the manager universally understood by most as 'Play me and I'll score for you'.

AWAY DAY TRAVELS – M

MANCHESTER CITY FC

Nickname – The Citizens / The Blues
Formed - 1880
Home Ground - Etihad Stadium
Capacity – *60,000 (Approximately)

*Sorry I cannot be more specific; I understand there's a programme of work currently underway at the stadium looking to increase the capacity to over 62,000

MOST MEMORABLE MATCH

MANCHESTER CITY 3 - 2 QPR (SUNDAY 13TH MAY 2012)

Even on a Sunday, the motorways in this country can be extremely busy and as a result, it took us over three hours to travel the 140 miles from Northampton to Manchester on the final Sunday of the 2011/2012 football season. Having made the journey up the M1 and M6 on numerous occasions we have a favourite stopping place: Keele services. Judging by the amount of replica QPR shirts being worn by people all around us, it's a popular stopping place for many other travelling QPR fans as well.

After the boys had finished running off steam playing football on a small grassed area adjoining the service station, we hopped back into the car and completed our journey north to Manchester.

A bit of a side issue, but one of the benefits of travelling with a regular group of friends is each of us has taken on specific roles. A great example of this is Terry Cadby who has a knack of finding us great places to eat. It's almost like he has a sixth sense, he has an excellent track record as over the years we've visited at a huge variety of 'eateries'. We've eaten homemade broths at small Delicatessens (Tottenham), West Indian jerk chicken (Watford), The Taste of the Taj curry house (QPR) and an array of fantastic fish and chips shops (Leicester, Nottingham, London and Wolverhampton) to name but a few. Perhaps the best measure of TC's continued search for culinary excellence is our ever-expanding waistlines.

On this occasion though, we'd allowed the three boys, Joshua, Ted and Matthew to select lunch today. The boys' food of choice? Somewhat predictably perhaps, a more mundane option of burger and chips.

Fate dictated that QPR were to face Manchester City away at the Etihad Stadium, on this, the final day of the football season. Little did we know that when the fixture list was published in June 2011 this match would have such an impact on the league winners and the final relegation place.

Clearly, QPR were favourites to join Blackburn Rovers and Wolverhampton Wanderers in the drop down to the Championship.

Bolton Wanderers looked to have the greatest chance of avoiding relegation. If, as expected, QPR lost and Bolton had beaten Stoke City then the Super Hoops would finish the season in 18th place, not good enough to stay in the Premiership.

The game at the Etihad saw Manchester City predictably start the game at a high tempo. Only a series of fine saves from QPR's Goalkeeper, Paddy Kenny prevented Manchester City from taking a well-deserved lead.

This was the sort of performance you'd expect from a team in QPR's perilous league position; a little disjointed and nervous in the opening minutes of the game, although City's failure to take an early lead meant QPR were slowly starting to grow in confidence.

Just at a time when QPR were beginning to gain a foothold in the game, Manchester City made the breakthrough - a fierce close range effort in the penalty box that Paddy Kenny could only parry, the ball spun into the net. 1-0 to Man City, Zabaleta on 39 mins.

Worse was to follow. The half-time news coming from the Britannia Stadium was grim, Bolton Wanderers had taken a 1-2 lead against Stoke City.

Had the situation not changed then QPR would be relegated with Bolton Wanderers securing 17th position in the league, safe for another season.

Much to our credit and far from accepting their fate, the Super Hoops used the half-time break to dust themselves down and continue the battle on the pitch in the second half.

I'm assuming that for all of the neutrals watching the match, the second period proved to be hugely entertaining. QPR equalised, then took the lead, and Joey Barton was sent-off, quite simply, the match had everything. To give you an indication of the pressure the QPR defence was under, at one point the corner count was 17-0 to Manchester City! Could QPR hold on?

The two Manchester clubs, City and United, had taken the fight for the Premier League title to the very last day of the 2011/2012 football season.

Despite both games having 4 minutes of extra time, the referee at the Stadium of Light (Sunderland v Manchester United) had already blown his whistle for full-time.

News started to filter through to the United players on the pitch that it looked like City had fallen at the last hurdle, as QPR were beating them 1-2 when the game moved into injury time. Some of the Utd. players were already celebrating, thinking it was all over at the Etihad.

Moments later however the smiles were wiped off the faces of the red half of Manchester. In an amazing close to the season, Manchester City had scored an equaliser in the 92nd minute. Unbelievably, there was still time for a fifth goal. The little Manchester City Striker, Sergio Aguero, drew deep on his reserves of energy, scoring the winning goal in the 94th minute.

In what proved to be the last few seconds of the game, he danced through the bemused QPR defence to score. His last gasp goal had secured the Premiership title for Manchester City, beating their arch-rivals Manchester United to the title on goal difference.

For all of the QPR fans watching this wonderful game of football at the Etihad, delight had turned to despair as we had no idea how the result had gone in the other relegation battle at the home of Stoke City; the Britannia Stadium.

A huge roar went up amongst the QPR fans when it became clear that Bolton had failed to win their final match and they, not us, had been relegated.

With that, the polite applause afforded to the Manchester City players and fans of the soon to be crowned champions by the travelling QPR fans turned into full-blown rendition of the famous City song "Blue Moon, you saw me standing alone".

An amazing day that I will always be glad to have been part of.

HISTORICAL INFORMATION

MAN CITY 2 - 2 QPR
(SATURDAY 25TH APRIL 1998)

In truth, the whole of the 1997-1998 season had been difficult for Queens Park Rangers. By mid-April we were running out of games, still woefully short of points as we looked to avoid being dumped into the third tier of

English football. It's hard to believe that back in 1998, Manchester City were also struggling to avoid being relegated. An unthinkable situation today; the current Premiership champions were facing the drop into Division 2.

It wasn't so much a question of losing games as we came to the end of the season, drawing matches was a real problem though. Indeed, 6 out of the last 7 league matches ended with QPR taking a single point from the game.

The penultimate fixture at Maine Road saw QPR draw 2-2, thanks to a superb own goal from the City player Jamie Pollock, a sublime piece of individual skill not seen since Paul Gascoigne's fabulous effort against the Scots at Wembley in 1996.

Facing his own goal, the City man skilfully intercepted a loose ball played in from the right, lifting the ball up and over 2 QPR players before calmly heading the ball past the advancing goalkeeper; brilliant!

The game finished 2-2. Adding to the poor chap's misfortune, thanks to his superb own goal QPR would go on to finish the season 1 point above Manchester City in the league. That single point was enough to keep QPR playing Division 1 football while relegating Manchester City to the Second Division.

City would eventually bounce back, the 'noisy neighbours' eclipsing the red half of the city by winning two Premiership titles in three years.

Before City made the move to the Etihad in 2003, their home for the previous 80 years had been at the old Maine Road stadium. A classic old football ground, although it was light years away from the calibre of Old Trafford - the home of the incredibly successful red half of the city Manchester United.

When the opportunity arose to buy the Commonwealth Games Stadium in Manchester and convert it into a fabulous football stadium, I'm assuming the City owners jumped at the chance.

I did visit Maine Road on one occasion, Lee Edmonds and I made the trip up north for a mid-week League Cup encounter; City v QPR.

We arrived early and parked up a short walk from the ground. What we'd failed to appreciate is that we had parked the car in Moss Side; it has the reputation for being one of the worst places in Manchester for violent crime. Worse was to follow, just for good measure, Lee and I proceeded to walk all around the local area searching for a chip shop!

City beat QPR 1-0 in a league cup fixture. Quite frankly, the best part of the match was the final whistle.

After the match, we arrived back at our car to find that an Audi parked immediately behind us had been vandalised. The car's side window had been smashed, with glass everywhere. I think it was Lee who spotted that the number plate on the damaged vehicle carried the name and telephone number of a London Garage, whereas ours was from Stockport. It could of course be coincidence, but ever since that trip I've always been careful of where I leave my car. I certainly would never leave anything in view that could identify our car as an 'away vehicle.'

Damage to vehicles is not just a problem in Manchester though. We'd used a small industrial estate as somewhere to park our car when attending home games at Loftus Road. Located off Wood Lane, pretty much opposite the main entrance to the BBC Television Centre. A busy, well-used and safe place to park? Sadly, not.

On this occasion, the vehicle parked immediately in front of ours had been vandalised. The owner of the car, a white Ford Orion, had obviously just arrived a few seconds before us. In utter disbelief he was wandering around his damaged car repeating "The b******s have nicked my bonnet."

QPR 4 - 0 MAN CITY
(SATURDAY 7TH MARCH 1992)

Another match against Manchester City worthy of mention dates back to the 7th March 1992, QPR 4 – 0 Manchester City (Ferdinand 2, Clive Wilson (pen), Barker).

I'd decided to take a rest from playing Saturday afternoon football for once to go to watch QPR v Man City with Terry Cadby and Lee Edmonds. When they both pulled out at the last minute, to avoid any further disappointment I decided to make the trip to Loftus Road from Northampton on my own.

Any football fan will tell you, Saturday afternoon football is a great way to spend time with your mates. On your own, it's still good, but without the usual crowd in tow, the pre-match build up is significantly quieter. With only the radio as company, the whole experience could have been a little flat.

I needn't have worried though, the 4-0 demolition of City and a fabulous home debut from Andy Impey made the whole trip worthwhile. Added to that, the bragging rights were mine for months!

MAN CITY 6 - 0 QPR
(SUNDAY 10TH MAY 2015)

The match summary for this one is easy to write and can be summed up by one word: pathetic. Over the years I have witnessed some terrible performances by the R's, none have been so gutless and dishonourable than this shocker at the Etihad though.

Our hapless defensive unit succumbed to the City attack as early as the 4th minute. Anyone watching knew from that moment on that QPR could be on the wrong end of a cricket-sized score.

QPR would go on to concede 6 goals without registering a response… shambolic! The only saving grace was that my wife Hayley had managed to secure a number of classy executive box tickets. If you have to watch the Rangers get annihilated, then seeing it through the bottom of a Guinness glass really does help.

AWAY DAY TRAVELS – M

MANCHESTER UTD FC

Nickname – The Red Devils
Formed - 1878
Home Ground - Old Trafford
Capacity – 75,731 (Season 2013-2014)

MOST MEMORABLE MATCH

MANCHESTER UTD. 1 - 4 QPR (WEDNESDAY 1ST JANUARY 1992)

Granted, this game goes back a few years now, but it still ranks as one of the best matches I've seen in my near 40 years of being a QPR supporter; albeit I watched it at home in the comfort of my own living-room.

No one gave us much of a chance against a United side starting to show the early signs of a team that would go on to dominate English Football for a generation.

Despite Manchester United being full of accomplished footballers, on the day they were out-thought and out-fought by a near flawless performance from the entire QPR team.

Goals from Andy Sinton and a blistering hat-trick from QPR's deeply religious, born-again Christian Dennis Bailey stunned the United faithful. In truth, Manchester United were simply swept away. The introduction of the precocious and amazingly talented teenager, Ryan Giggs did little to help their cause. Well before the end of the contest, the QPR fans would acknowledge the superb performance of the QPR striker by singing "Dennis Bailey, Hallelujah, Hallelujah."

From United's perspective, the totally unexpected and heavy home defeat at the hands of QPR would prove to be a defining point for their whole season. Results elsewhere meant that the Red Devils would lose top spot in the league. Prior to the QPR fixture Utd. had been 2 points clear at the top of the table with 2 games in hand. The defeat pushed them down into second place, a single point behind the eventual champions: Leeds United.

In truth, this was another great time in recent history to be a QPR fan, with Gerry Francis at the helm; we were a popular team playing amongst the elite of English football. Hard fought victories against so-called glamorous or more illustrious opponents earned us a grudging respect for our quality and style of play from fans of other clubs.

Since the introduction of the Premier League, we've all had to pay for the privilege of watching SKY TV's excellent live, High Definition coverage of English football. However, back in the early 1990s things were a little different. The format of matches covered live on television had hardly changed since the switch from black and white to colour TV years beforehand.

Although it's now some 23 years after the event I can still clearly remember a classic piece of television captured during ITV's build-up to the Manchester United v QPR fixture being broadcast live from Old Trafford.

It mattered little that it was a free to watch programme and the production and budget levels were significantly below today's standards, ITV still managed to capture a key part of the pre-match build up; an interview with Alex Ferguson.

I will never forget, when answering a question from the match commentator about what QPR should expect from his United team that day, he replied through the smuggest smile, "QPR will have come here expecting us to attack, we wouldn't want to disappoint them."

Such a shame that there's no footage of the moment Dennis Bailey went to the Manchester United dressing room to ask Mr Ferguson to sign the match ball following the 1-4 demolition of his United side!

Another classic from the same game was the obvious discomfort of the former United hero, Denis Law. As a member of the commentary team he was obviously being asked to share his worldly knowledge with the millions of TV viewers as to why United were being thrashed so easily. He knew full well they'd completely underestimated QPR and were now paying the price. His constant squirming in his seat was a great piece of television, the fact that he couldn't answer the question meant that every time he was asked I felt the need to shout the answer for him: "Cos you're s**t" …happy days!

Much to the amusement of many football fans, Manchester United would eventually finish the 1991-1992 campaign in second place in the league, the last season in the old Division 1 to 4 format. The following August saw the introduction of the Premier League, something that the red half of Manchester would go on to almost make their own, winning the title on 13 occasions between 1993 and 2013. The most significant difference between the United side that lost the league title in 1992 and the early years of the serial silverware winners from 1993 onwards was one Eric Cantona.

For all of their obvious quality, the 1992 United side still needed a Talisman, a focal point for the whole team. United would finally get the missing piece of their jigsaw puzzle on 26th November 1992.

The signing of the mercurial Frenchman proved to be the missing ingredient, turning a talented side into a hugely successful one, winning multiple English and European crowns.

It can be no coincidence that over the years, many good clubs have assembled fantastic squads. The truly great ones have all had an exceptional player leading the team's charge for trophies. Over the years Liverpool had Kenny Dalglish or Ian Rush; Arsenal had Ian Wright, Denis Bergkamp or Thierry Henry. Manchester United now had their man.

Old Trafford can be an intimidating place to be, with many underperforming opponents choking in front of over 75,000 fans, effectively beating the opposition before a ball has been kicked. Not on New Year's Day 1992 though, a day that will live long in the memory of lots of QPR fans.

In hindsight, I wish I'd been at Old Trafford to witness the humiliation of Manchester United. Sadly, for me, I cannot claim to be one of the few who watched this wonderful game live. I could give you a list of excuses as to why I couldn't get there, although in truth had I really have wanted to I'm sure I could have got tickets.

The regret of not going to Manchester to see the 1-4 drubbing of United would work in my favour a few weeks later though, oddly enough against the other Manchester side: City.

HISTORICAL INFORMATION

QPR 4 - 0 MANCHESTER UNITED
(TUESDAY 19TH APRIL 1977)

Before I get onto the historical details of matches and events gone by, I'd just like to add for the record that I'm sitting here early on Sunday morning following our 0-2 home defeat by Manchester United on Saturday 17th January 2015. It was a master class of moaning and whining by the entire United team. This isn't a case of sour grapes as in truth they had probably done just enough to win the game anyway.

However, I do find it extremely difficult to tolerate highly paid professional footballers demonstrating such poor behaviour.

Sadly, one of the biggest culprits on the day was Manchester United and England captain, Wayne Rooney. It seemed Mr Rooney was whining about everything; probably including the weather.

Surely if the match officials talked to the players before kick-off to warn them that dissent in any form would attract a booking, the problem would soon disappear?

As a football fan who regularly attends matches it's obvious that referees are clearly trigger happy when issuing yellow cards to known tough tackling individuals throughout the football leagues. However, they then fail to warn or book players who continually argue the toss about every decision given against their team. A tactic most fans will know is designed purely to intimidate and influence future decisions… come on referees, wake-up!

The match was yet another example of how QPR had walked away from games this season empty handed when perhaps they might have won at least a point.

Over the years QPR have often given a good account of themselves when playing Manchester United, mostly with little or nothing to show for it.

One regular feature of the fixtures though were the battles between United's Mark Hughes and QPR's Alan MacDonald. They became legendary! You got the impression that some of the tussles may have been settled in the car park after the game, such was the venom flowing from the two players throughout the entire passage of play. Often resembling little more than bare knuckle fighting, most match officials seemed to be happy to let both players sort out their differences on the field of play.

Even when the late, great Alan MacDonald didn't feature we had a ready-made replacement in Darren Peacock. I remember him putting in his first challenge on Mark Hughes, a sort of "Macca said to say hello" tackle where the United forward flew so high, he had to wait for permission from air traffic control before he could land!

Another fond memory I have is from 19th April 1977, where under the floodlights at Loftus Road in front of 28,848 fans, QPR hammered United 4-0. Goals from Don Givens, Eddie Kelly and 2 from Peter Eastoe secured the victory in a completely one sided affair.

Perhaps, some of the shine was taken off this result as Manchester Utd. were only days away from taking part in an FA Cup semi-final.

The heavy defeat inflicted at Loftus Road proved not to have left any lasting damage as the Manchester club would go onto secure victory in the semi-final and then the final itself, beating Liverpool 2-1 at Wembley Stadium.

I have travelled to Old Trafford on two occasions, both ending in defeats for QPR.

The first was in November, 2008. QPR lost 1-0 in the Carling Cup. Getting knocked out of the cup proved to be a minor detail, much more significant was a serious knee injury suffered by Akos Buzsaky. Our season ground to a halt after losing such a skilful and influential player.

The second was a 2-0 defeat in the Premiership in April 2012. When you travel up to Manchester to watch your team play, especially when you take your young son along, it works out to be an expensive day. That's not a complaint as I simply love being in a position to visit these superb stadia with my friends and family. It's a sad fact that my son, Joshua, has been to Old Trafford on more occasions than many so-called Manchester United fans from all around the UK. What I do find hard to swallow is that our chance of getting anything from this game was effectively over within 15 minutes of the kick-off, the referee awarding a penalty to United when serial diver, Ashley Young, took a theatrical tumble in the QPR penalty box.

Subsequent TV replays clearly show what everyone apart from the referee already knew, Shaun Derry hadn't touched him. What I found most disappointing was the ref (Lee Mason) had the whistle in his mouth and was pointing to the penalty spot before the player had hit the ground, almost as if he'd decided to award a penalty to United in the car on the way to the game.

To add insult to injury, the QPR player was sent-off and despite the video evidence seemingly proving there was no contact, the sending off was upheld by the FA.

As I've already stated, intimidation of match officials should be stamped out. All they have to defend themselves are two cards, one yellow, and the other red. So why aren't they used more often?

Other sports (rugby, cricket, hockey etc.) implement strict rules and punishment for dissent, surely it wouldn't be that difficult for football to follow suit?

Sadly, watching my son Joshua progress through football's junior leagues, at the age of 12 there's already ample evidence that some youngsters are following the example of the highly paid professional footballers in the game's less favourable side.

I have one final point to make before I move on to the next away day experience - diving!

When a player takes a tumble in an attempt to 'win' a free kick or penalty and the referee correctly identifies that no contact was made, I love to see a player being cautioned for diving. Seconds after rolling around on the floor in apparent agony, in a modern-day sporting miracle the 'injured' player jumps to his feet to protest his innocence, the crippling injury long forgotten.

FA CUP 4TH ROUND 2017 – MANCHESTER UNITED VS. WIGAN ATHLETIC

Purely by chance, I'm just checking the last few pages of 'QPR ADT' before I return the manuscript to the publisher. The half-time whistle has just gone in the Sunday evening Manchester United vs. Wigan Athletic FA Cup tie. I have to say that Wayne Rooney has again been the bitter, caustic and argumentative plonker described earlier in this section. Now, I cannot second guess what the Man Utd No. 10 was trying to say to the referee, I can only guess that the irate looking rant and flapping arms mean that Mr Rooney wasn't checking on the man in black's wellbeing! It would seem that old habits die hard.

AWAY DAY TRAVELS – N
NEWCASTLE UTD FC

Nickname – The Magpies
Formed - 1892
Home Ground - St James' Park
Capacity – 52,405

HISTORICAL INFORMATION

I found out recently that I have distant family connections with the city of Newcastle and the surrounding area. This makes it much easier for me to confess to people I had a soft spot for the Magpies in the mid-1990s. It's not that I ever thought about ditching QPR, it was just refreshing to see the usual suspects in the race for the Premiership title outplayed and beaten by a Newcastle team full of skill and enthusiasm.

The manager during this time, Kevin Keegan, had returned to his former club some 8 years after he'd last played a professional game for the Magpies. Under his stewardship United's style of play won them many admirers. A comment from that era which has stuck with me is, "If you score four goals against them, United would back themselves to score five."

In my opinion, at a domestic level, very rarely do a team who play such an open and attacking style of football actually go on to win anything. The more defensive-minded teams that play a quick, counter-attacking game or have enough money to buy players that dominate every position on the field (or both!), somewhat unsurprisingly tend to be more successful.

However, in the first few weeks of 1996, it seemed that their irrepressible brand of hugely entertaining football had all but secured their first league title in the top tier of English football since 1927.

Indeed, at the end of January, with two thirds of the season already complete, Newcastle sat proudly on top of the Premiership table, some 9 points clear of the teams in second and third place (Liverpool and

Manchester United respectively). The added cushion of also having a game in-hand surely meant they'd go on to win the league? Sadly not.

A toxic combination of nerves and the crushing weight of the Geordie fans' expectations saw Newcastle spectacularly implode. The ashen faced Keegan lost his cool (and in most people's opinion, the title) when almost foaming at the mouth he gave the passionate "I would love it if we beat them (Manchester United), love it" TV interview… game over.

The Manchester United manager, Alex Ferguson, obviously well-versed in the black art of mind games, had been sniping at the Newcastle manager for weeks, which in my opinion, made him at least partly responsible for the incredible meltdown experienced on Tyneside.

Unbelievably, Manchester United would catch and then overtake Newcastle to ensure the Magpies' wait for the top division's league title continues.

Newcastle would again finish in second place in 1997. Had they won the title as they should have done in 1996, I'm convinced they'd have rivalled Manchester United for domestic honours for a generation.

HISTORICAL INFORMATION

QPR 5 - 5 NEWCASTLE UNITED (SATURDAY 22ND SEPTEMBER 1984)

I've been fortunate to see QPR play on numerous occasions since visiting Loftus Road for the first time in September 1976. In all of the years since, I've only missed a handful of games that would feature anywhere close to the top of a list of 'Classic Encounters'.

One such match against Newcastle in September 1984 turned out to be a 10-goal thriller, 'classic' enough to appear on anyone's list.

Although I didn't attend this fixture, it is one of those occasions where I can tell you where I was and what I was doing on the afternoon of 22/09/84.

An unbelievable game of football, played by two teams who it seemed had absolutely no inclination to defend their goal throughout the entire 90 minutes of football.

In 1984, QPR had only recently completed a major overhaul of the Loftus Road stadium and the playing staff. The all-weather, plastic/synthetic pitch was still in use and Guinness were the club's main sponsor. I'd just turned 18 and had recently discovered the most famous drink to come out of Ireland just happens to be my drink of choice, perhaps that's why I was so proud to wear the fantastic Adidas shirt with 'Guinness' as the club sponsor.

Having seen highlights from this classic encounter on several occasions, I still can't believe the number of empty seats especially in the South Africa Road stand. Such a disappointment when you consider what happened over the course of the match.

Having left games early myself, I can honestly sympathise with QPR fans who'd seen the visitors race into a 4 goal lead, perhaps having decided that at 0-4 down they'd seen enough, and they simply left.

What happened next though was quite astonishing, something that had every QPR fan watching or listening on the edge of their seats. A fantastic comeback saw QPR score three goals in quick succession (score: QPR 3 – 4 Newcastle).

Somewhat inevitably perhaps, with QPR chasing a dramatic equaliser; Newcastle tore up the script; scoring the 8th goal of the game (QPR 3-5 Newcastle).

Surely now QPR's spirit had been broken? Absolutely not, goals 9 and 10 went to the Super Hoops. The dramatic equaliser scored by Gary Micklewhite epitomised the 'never-say-die' attitude demonstrated by every member of the QPR team.

Bursting into the penalty box and with the clock ticking down to full-time, Micklewhite blasted the ball beyond the Magpies' keeper; unbelievably from 0-4 down QPR had achieved the seemingly impossible, snatching a draw from the jaws of defeat (Final Score: QPR 5-5 Newcastle).

HE WHO LAUGHS LAST......
Stanley really ought not to rub it in so much—but Malcolm Macdonald HAD rather over-done the criticism of Rangers before the away game at Newcastle and Stan HAD scored a beautiful goal in the 89th minute. So...
(Photo: John Brough).

Subtle Stanley! Bowles' 'in-your-face' style of goal celebration. Believe it or not, Stan and the Newcastle No. 9 (Malcolm MacDonald) didn't get on.

HISTORICAL INFORMATION

NEWCASTLE UNITED 1 - 2 QPR
(SATURDAY 16TH OCTOBER 1993)

In October 1993, QPR travelled to the North East to play a Newcastle side beginning to show the signs of becoming a top Premiership team.

On the day though, a QPR side, playing in a strange orange away kit, defeated Kevin Keegan's Newcastle, 1-2. A totally dominant performance (and goal) from QPR's Les Ferdinand and a superb second goal from his striking partner, Bradley Allen was enough to silence the home fans.

A thoroughly entertaining game. QPR could have easily won by a wider margin, with Ferdinand hitting a post after being put through on goal by the former England Captain, Ray Wilkins. Newcastle added to the drama of the match, missing a last-minute penalty.

Such a fabulous all-round performance from Ferdinand probably helped to secure his £6 million transfer to Newcastle in 1995.

HISTORICAL INFORMATION

NEWCASTLE UNITED 1 - 1 QPR
(WEDNESDAY 30TH SEPTEMBER 2009)

My only visit to St. James' Park took place on 30th September 2009, a 1-1 draw secured against that season's eventual winners of the Championship.

A goal from Ben Watson gave QPR the lead, although in truth a Newcastle equaliser always looked probable.

I found the whole trip superb, travelling up to Newcastle with Terry Cadby and Lee Edmonds is always full of mickey taking and banter. Arriving in plenty of time to mix with the home fans, we found the Newcastle supporters very approachable, knowledgeable and happy to talk football. Terry even found time to get a 5 Star recommendation from a fan on a local Chinese Restaurant; his ability to find us good food whilst on our travels is legendary.

Once in the stadium, we took our seats. The superb view of the pitch (and the surrounding area) added to the sense of occasion.

A great night, even allowing for the fact that a mid-week away game at Newcastle made it an incredibly late night. Indeed, our journey home was made even worse by being delayed on the motorway for 'Bridge Cleaning' Grrrrrrrr. If I hadn't seen it, I wouldn't have believed it!

We eventually arrived back in Northampton at 2:30am.

AWAY DAY TRAVELS – N

NORTHAMPTON TOWN FC

Nickname – The Cobblers
Formed – 1897
Home Ground - Sixfields Stadium
Capacity – 7,653

HISTORICAL INFORMATION

When I first began to worship anything and everything QPR in the mid-1970s, I very quickly became a total optimist.

With this most positive of outlooks, in my mind it was only a matter of time before QPR were confirmed as the best team in the world.

Not just a fluffy notion, as results on the field of play seemed to suggest we were on the edge of something REALLY special. We'd already beaten one of the top German sides in a pre-season friendly, most impressive when you consider that in 1975, Germany were the current FIFA World Champions.

In my opinion, any question that we were the best team in England had already been addressed. The first 7 days of the 1975-76 campaign saw QPR easily beat Liverpool 2-0, draw against Aston Villa 1-1 then totally demolish the current league champions, Derby County, 1-5 at the Baseball Ground.

My dream of QPR being named as the world's finest team had effectively ended in 1977, with QPR losing the UEFA Cup quarter final, second leg, on penalties to the Greek team AEK Athens. This after taking a 3-0 lead into the match from the home leg… only QPR!

During those heady days where QPR could (and often did) beat anyone, if someone had told me that some 26 years later we'd be playing my local team, Northampton Town, I'd probably have laughed at them.

In my mind, playing each other in the league simply shouldn't have been possible. The mid 1970s saw QPR playing in the top flight while the

Cobblers were struggling in the 4th Division. Any meaningful fixture between the two sides would surely result in nothing more than a cricket score, a huge win for the R's. The reality of course, was completely different.

Most disturbing of all was the fact that after years of decline, QPR had now joined Northampton Town, playing their football matches in the English lower leagues.

MOST MEMORABLE MATCH

NORTHAMPTON TOWN 2 - 1 QPR (TUESDAY 21ST AUGUST 2001)

Our first encounter for many years was indeed in the opening round of a Cup competition (League Cup). No easy victory for the R's here though as the match ended in a 2-1 victory for the Cobblers. The result proved to be a rude awakening for those fans, myself included, who thought we were good enough for a run in the cup.

On the night, it certainly looked as if the majority of the 4,638 fans attending the match were QPR supporters. A sea of blue and white scarves were worn by hordes of youngsters, their parents obviously taking advantage of the warm summer evenings and the school holidays.

As we took our seats, most fans around where I sat also seemed to believe a QPR victory was inevitable. Everything seemed to be progressing to plan especially when, following a promising start, QPR took the lead in the 16th minute.

Not exactly a totally dominant performance, although QPR did have the greater possession and went on to create a number of opportunities to score that vital second goal.

As is often the case, a single goal and heaps of possession is no absolute guarantee of victory.

Sure enough, with the end of the scheduled 90 minutes of play less than 2 minutes away, in a script looking increasingly like it had been written by a Northampton Town supporter; the Cobblers equalised.

In an instant, from being a side looking like they had more than enough about them to hold on for victory, QPR simply fell apart. It was no great surprise when in the second period of extra-time, QPR conceded another goal. With little time to reply, Rangers looked every bit a beaten side... and so it proved to be.

I cannot begin to describe the total and utter bone crushing feeling of losing to the Cobblers. The final safety net had been removed. The no-brainer, the line in the sand, all gone. What next? After this, in my mind anything was possible. Oddly enough, this result helped me re-evaluate and reset what it means to support QPR.

Just for the record, in my opinion it would take a fixture early in 2003 for QPR to hit rock bottom and for me to hit my absolute zero in terms of belief that QPR would ever come good again. At this time, it would have been incredibly easy for me to stop going to see QPR play altogether.

In case you're wondering, the fixture that pushed me to the very limit of my patience was a Second Division league match that oddly enough we would go on to win; QPR 1 - 0 Stockport County, Saturday 4th January 2003.

It was a bitterly cold day where, despite being wrapped up against the very worst of the elements, the circulation to my hands and feet had all but ceased well before half time. It took me a while to realise that the reason I had no blood flow was simple, there was nothing to cheer for. Nothing to get me up out of my seat, nothing for me to clap or get excited about; absolutely nothing to get the blood pumping. Then in the 89th minute we were awarded a penalty, duly converted by the QPR Striker, Kevin Gallen. I was so cold, to this day I firmly believe my hands and feet were all but clinically dead. Certainly, there was no chance of me celebrating the goal in what I'm sure was our only shot on goal! A strange experience when you're glad your team has won but you can't shake the feeling of 'What the bloody hell am I doing here'?

HISTORICAL INFORMATION

Over a couple of seasons early in the new millennium, QPR and Northampton Town would play each other regularly both in league and cup competitions; the Cobblers almost always coming out on top. Indeed, QPR have only managed a single victory from the last 10 encounters with the Cobblers stretching back to the late 1950s.

When, for example, Northampton Town handed QPR a two-goal lead in a league fixture dating back to February 2002, most of us kept the champagne on ice! Being two goals up, most football fans might understandably believe their team would go on to take 3 points; not QPR though. With the opposition singing "You'll never beat the Cobblers" ringing in our ears, they'd score 2 quick goals to claim a point.

I'm guessing of course, but popular opinion would probably have me down as a Manchester United fan. After all, living within a few miles of the place you were born, in my case Northampton, and not supporting your local team has offered the likes of United rich pickings over the years. It's not that I would like to see most youngsters wearing the blue and white hooped shirts of QPR when playing football in just about every park throughout the country, far from it. I honestly believe that the passion felt by supporters for 'their' club is diluted by the weight of sheer numbers. Such a shame that the love of the 'Beautiful Game' can become so stunted and shallow.

I must admit to having a huge amount of respect for the younger generation of football fans who support their local team (or any of the less fashionable clubs). I honestly believe by simply choosing not to follow their peers by supporting the Manchester Uniteds, Arsenals, Chelseas or Liverpools of this world, then they will see a greater variety of life as a football fan.

In my opinion, not being able to buy a QPR shirt from a Sports Direct retail outlet is a clear indication that my club is unfashionable: fantastic! What it does mean though is when you do see a youngster wearing a QPR shirt, you can be reasonably sure that it's been purchased from the club shop, clearly demonstrating that he or she has actually been to the ground to see a match; something that most followers of the so-called elite of English football wouldn't ever have achieved.

I will admit that I would always want the Cobblers to do well. However, it's true to say that would never be anywhere near as well as QPR.

For most of the last 40 years Northampton Town have spent a majority of their time languishing in the fourth tier of English football, occasionally producing talented individuals who have proved themselves to be capable of playing at the very top of club and international football. The first and most obvious player to mention is former Northampton Town, Liverpool and England Defender Phil Neal.

A Liverpool legend of the 1970s and 1980s, winning numerous European and UEFA cup winners medals as well as domestic league titles, FA and League cup winners medals by the bucket load, Phil signed for Northampton Town in 1967, moving to Liverpool FC in October in 1974. For a local lad from Irchester (Northamptonshire) Phil's career was second to none in professional football.

Another former Cobblers player to have recorded a number of successes during his time as a professional footballer, including 6 appearances for England at full international level, is John Gregory. This, along with the 4 years he spent playing at Loftus Road meant that in my opinion he did very well for himself. During his time at QPR he would play in an FA Cup final and was an integral part of the 1982-83 Division 2 championship winning team.

Whereas it is true to say John wouldn't go on to record anywhere near the number or variety of winners medals that Phil Neal did during his playing career, an honour missing from Phil Neal's illustrious career is the fact that he didn't ever play for QPR!

AWAY DAY TRAVELS – N

NORWICH CITY FC

**Nickname – The Canaries
Formed - 1902
Home Ground - Carrow Road
Capacity – 27,244**

MOST MEMORABLE MATCH

NORWICH CITY 3 - 2 QPR (SATURDAY 17TH APRIL 1976)

Easter Saturday 1976 - this away defeat at Norwich City was the first time I had been left feeling utterly crushed by the result of a football match. Sadly, it's a feeling that I now appreciate is all too familiar for QPR fans.

The run-up to the fixture at Carrow Road had been an excellent one for QPR. Having won 13 of the last 15 matches, a victory against Norwich City would almost seal the Division 1 League Title.

I remember as a 9-year-old, sitting in the back of my dad's tiny Fiat 850 Sports Coupe on the way back from a short family holiday, trying to listen to the second half commentary on the radio.

Unlike the digital sound quality afforded to today's lucky travellers, back in the mid-1970s radio commentary was a hit and miss affair, the BBC broadcasting their flagship Saturday afternoon sports programme on the notoriously unpredictable Medium Wave band. A bad situation was made even worse, as in common with most family cars of the day, my dad's little Fiat had a single speaker. Sounds laughable today, but at the time it proved to be most frustrating to anyone who actually wanted to listen to the radio, especially in the back!

To be honest, I could hardly hear a thing. The amount of times I asked my parents to turn the radio up brought a warning from my dad that the radio was up as loud as it was going to get, any more moaning and it would be turned off.

Never was it made clearer to me that my parents just didn't 'get' football. Worse was to follow, I groaned a little too loudly when QPR went 1-0 down... I received my second and final warning.

When the fantastic Dave Thomas (QPR) danced through the Norwich City defence to score the equaliser, I punched the air in delight. A gut reaction that my brother (a Liverpool fan at the time) instantly reported to my parents. "Grow up Simon" came the instruction from the front seats.

They really had no idea that this wasn't the only reaction to the equalising goal. When confirmation came through from the BBC commentary team at Carrow Road that QPR had indeed drawn level, there were firecrackers and screamers going off inside my head. Had they seen the broad smile and glazed expression on my face, they probably would have guessed that I'd all but imploded and the radio would have been switched off for the remainder of the journey home.

Elation quickly turned to desolation though as Norwich scored a second; Peter Morris hit an unstoppable shot that flew past Phil Parkes, the QPR Goalkeeper beaten from well outside of the penalty box. It was one of those annoying occasions where you know if a player like Morris chooses that day to score the best of his career goals, the writing is on the wall. Indeed, it was soon made absolutely clear that on the day good fortune favoured Norwich City, their third, and decisive goal looked to be a mile offside.

Back on the M5, as the Ingram family travelled back from our short break in North Devon, my mood lifted a little as QPR came back to make it 3-2. However, this thread of hope was quickly extinguished as I seem to remember the QPR legend, Stan Bowles, being sent-off for a cynical foul, most likely born out of frustration.

Despite all our best efforts, Norwich held firm to take the game and the championship away from QPR.

I was close to tears, in an attempt to avoid the inevitable telling off from my parents I simply slid down in my seat and pretended to be asleep.

Liverpool would eventually go on to take first place by the narrowest of margins: a single point.

As for the scorer of Norwich City's crucial second goal, Peter Morris? Our paths would cross while he managed Northampton Town, my local team, for a spell late in the 1990s.

I love to watch a game of football, most especially in between Christmas and New Year. The excesses of the festive period are all blown away by the typically cold and crispy conditions. Added to that, no one seems to be rushed as the majority of people are relaxed and in good spirits after several days away from work. With more time to burn before returning to their regular 9 to 5, watching football from the stands is a great way to spend a couple of hours during the winter holidays.

A word of caution though, be careful if you decide to wear an expensive Christmas gift that really doesn't belong at a football match.

During the late 2000s the four members of the Ingram family decided to go to the Boxing Day fixture, my wife Hayley was sitting next to our son Joshua while he sat struggling to eat a hot chicken pie. Both Hayley and I had offered to help, Josh was having none of it though, at 5 years of age he was determined to complete the tricky exercise himself. There he sat, the plastic fork almost bent double as he tried to remove a large piece of chicken, steaming in the freezing conditions. It sat almost completely embedded in the soggy pastry, covered in a deliciously thick gravy.

Hayley and I could do nothing, as like a cork from a bottle, the piece of chicken suddenly broke free. The fork bent double giving the lump of food the momentum it needed to sail through the air, hitting the gentleman sitting directly in front of us squarely between the shoulder blades. The back of his brand-new cashmere coat was splattered with chicken pie.

With the innocence of youth, Joshua leaned forward to scrape the food from the man's coat. A look of total bewilderment appeared on Joshua's face as both Hayley and I stopped him and then tried to explain in a hushed tone that it was better to leave it to dry first and not to say anything to the man…oops!

On this occasion though, with no QPR game scheduled and with the Cobblers' game being postponed due to a frozen pitch, a lifelong friend and fellow 'Ranger', Lee Edmonds and I decided to travel the 10 miles along the A45 to go and watch Rushden and Diamonds play. So had the Northampton Town Manager, Peter Morris. He'd obviously taken the opportunity to watch another locally based team whose match had survived the big freeze.

By a strange twist of fate, he ended up sitting directly behind me in the main stand.

It may have been the best part of 24 years since he scored 'that' goal, but the memory was still so vivid in my mind, I had to move seats to avoid taking him to task. Yet again, a great example of me carrying a grudge!

HISTORICAL INFORMATION

NORWICH CITY 3 - 0 QPR
(SATURDAY 26TH APRIL 2008)

Luigi De Canio had taken over as Manager at QPR in late October 2007. Some of the football played under his stewardship was the best I had seen at QPR for years. Added to his refreshingly open attacking style of play, the players at the club seemed to be at the right place at the right time. A mixture of skill, tenacity and courage, in short, the sort of players Di Canio needed.

The partnership of Akos Buzsaky and Rowan Vine added real class and a cutting edge few teams could live with.

By the end of April 2008, rumours were coming out of Loftus Road thick and fast that Di Canio and his family were homesick. Results started to go against us and the manager didn't seem to have the answer. All too soon the little Italian decided QPR wasn't for him and he returned home, to be sadly missed by QPR fans.

This match is obviously not about the result, the team looked fragile and vulnerable without a 'Plan B'. It's more to announce that by visiting Carrow Road in 2008, I finally managed to lay the ghost of 1976 to rest. I'm still no fan of Norwich City, but have to say I've now made my peace with the club.

AWAY DAY TRAVELS – N
NOTTINGHAM FOREST FC

Nickname – Forest or The Reds
Formed – 1865
Home Ground - The City Ground
Capacity – 30,576

MOST MEMORABLE MATCH

NOTTINGHAM FOREST 1 - 1 QPR (SATURDAY 28TH AUGUST 1999)

Sadly, not even on the occasion of my 33rd birthday were QPR able to change the fact that in over 20 attempts, we have never beaten Forest away from Loftus Road (a statistic that stands to this day).

Not that Lee Edmonds and I travelled up to Nottingham with anything other than total belief that we'd finish the day 3 points better off. Even the fact that Forest had just signed the former England international and goal-scoring machine Ian Wright on loan from Arsenal could not change that. Indeed, our faith in QPR and their ability to beat anyone was so strong that we even stopped to pick-up Matthew Bulliman (a life-long Forest fan) on the way.

Matthew, Lee and I were all working at Cosworth Engineering at the time, so a QPR win was vital to secure the Monday morning bragging rights.

Lee's legendary lack of anything resembling humility had him singing an amended version of the chorus of the INXS song "Baby Don't Cry" changed to "Matty Don't Cry", he happily sang at the top of his voice at regular intervals during the trip north…what a star!

With Terry Cadby busy doing other things on the day, Matty was able to direct us to a selection of the best eateries that Nottingham had to offer.

Typically, without TC's overwhelming desire to sample as much food from around the globe as possible, somewhat predictably we settled for fish and chips.

The match itself was a hard-fought draw in a really good atmosphere. The Forest fans were obviously loving the fact that Ian Wright was playing for them and sang his name repeatedly, "Ian Wright, Wright, Wright", something that the QPR fans changed to "Ian W**k, W**k, W**k."

Wright would go on to have the last laugh though, scoring Forest's goal in a match that finished 1-1. Although he was wearing a broad smile, his hand gesture to the QPR fans suggested that he hadn't appreciated our singing.

On the journey home, Matty had tried to sing his own version of "Eddo, Don't Cry" until it was politely pointed out by Mr Edmonds that it was a long walk home!

HISTORICAL INFORMATION

NOTTINGHAM FOREST 5 - 0 QPR (THURSDAY 26ᵀᴴ JANUARY 2010)

This is the game that has finished my desire to make the relatively short journey from Northampton to Nottingham to see QPR play at the City Ground ever again.

On a bitterly cold night in January 2010, a QPR team that had promised so much just 3 months earlier offered nothing against a Forest team that must have finished the match thinking over the course of 90 minutes they had become super stars. To say we were lucky to get nil is understating just how poorly we played.

On the plus side, there have been plenty of fine performances at Loftus Road since our total capitulation at the City Ground. Indeed, arguably the best display of the 2013-2014 season saw QPR thrash Forest 5-2 in front of our home fans shortly before our play-off final victory at Wembley.

One final story to tell before I move onto the next venue. In the late 1970s, under the management of Brian Clough and Peter Taylor, Forest would start their almost total domination of English football and the European Cup.

Promoted to the old Division One at the end of the 1976-77 season, nobody could have foreseen just how big Forest were about to become.

I'd been fortunate enough to become a regular member of the Weston Athletic boy's football club in the mid-70s. Although I was only 9 years of age, I had become sufficiently skilled to play in the Under 13s. Eric Berlin, the manager of Weston Athletic poured his heart and soul into the club. A chap who was totally motivated by his football club, he took it upon himself to organise a mid-summer visit to see Nottingham Forest train.

What great memories I have of watching the future champions of England (and Europe) training by the river Trent.

At the end of the day's training session, we were allowed to stand and wait for the players by the main entrance to ask for their autographs. The first of the two players I remember in particular was the seasoned defender, Larry Lloyd. His memorable action? To my horror, he jabbed another player in the b******s sending the hapless man to the floor in a crumpled heap. Laughing as he walked off, muttering, "They should be hard by now."

The second was a young member of the reserves, who initially tried talking me out of taking his signature. The player? Steve Burke. By a strange twist of fate, Burke would sign for QPR in September 1979.

After a fairly promising start to his career in West London, his influence faded. Even so, he made a substitute appearance for QPR in the 1982 FA Cup Final.

AWAY DAY TRAVELS – W

WATFORD FC

Nickname – The Hornets
Formed – 1881 (Watford Rovers)
Home Ground - Vicarage Road
Capacity – 20,877

MOST MEMORABLE MATCH

WATFORD 0 - 2 QPR
(SUNDAY 30TH APRIL 2011)

A fabulous day, performance and result against a lively and difficult opponent, although the FA managed to tarnish the occasion with a threat of a points deduction hanging over our heads. The wrangle over a possible procedural error in the registration and subsequent 'ownership' of the QPR player Alejandro Faurlin was still several days away from being resolved.

QPR had effectively already won promotion to the Premiership. This 0 – 2 victory against Watford ensured that we would go up as Champions. What a season to be a fan! 'Come On You R's!'

Somewhat fittingly, the first of our two goals was scored by Adel Taarabt, our player of the season by a country mile.

Although the QPR players and management had all performed spectacularly throughout the season to achieve promotion, in a team full of grit and determination, he alone ensured the league title was won with style. For anyone wishing to check to see just how influential he was on the 2010-11 team, take a look at that season's Boxing Day fixture against Swansea. Simply sublime.

A player capable of extreme highs and lows, a huge debt of thanks is owed to Neil Warnock for man-managing Taarabt to perfection. Warnock obviously understood that if you were to get anywhere close to the best out of Taarabt, he had to be indulged. No tracking back or making life difficult for your opponents for him. A popular rumour amongst QPR fans at the time was, if any member of the QPR team passed to him in our own half, they would be fined. The QPR management team knew that if he practised his brand of trickery too deep and lost the ball, there would be little time for the QPR midfield and defence to prevent the opposition from creating a goal scoring opportunity.

I'm only guessing, but I would think that there could have been a number of bruised egos amongst the playing staff at QPR that season with Warnock going out of his way to ensure a happy and therefore productive Taarabt.

With the freedom to simply go and create havoc on the field of play, pretty much everything we threw at Watford seemed to originate from him.

Perhaps somewhat inevitably, the QPR No. 7 scored the opening goal of the game, bringing his total to 19 for the season.

At first glance, his goal on 77 minutes looked every inch a tap-in at the near post. It's only when you watch the replay you see that he had to adjust his body in mid-air to ensure his shot was on target and hit with sufficient power to beat the opposition's goalkeeper.

Although QPR scored a second goal through Tommy Smith on 90 minutes, the game was already over as a contest. Still, no harm in celebrating another goal.

AWAY DAY TRAVELS – W
WEMBLEY STADIUM

Old… *In use since 1923, the old stadium closed its doors to the public for the final time in October 2000. The once mighty home of English football, sporting the iconic twin towers, was finally to be replaced. I was fortunate to visit Wembley on a number of occasions. I was saddened to hear that the old twin towers couldn't be saved.*

And the new…

The Football Association made a huge financial commitment deciding to level the old stadium and rebuild a fabulous, all-new facility, fit to showcase football in this country for many decades to come.

The new stadium proved to be every bit as majestic as the original. The spectacular stadium reopened in March 2007. A stylish and imposing modern day classic, set against the backdrop of the North London skyline, it served as a focal point and rightful home for English football.

The new Wembley is without doubt a magnificent arena, although its status as the UK's premier football facility is regularly being challenged.

Numerous clubs across the country have refurbished their existing home grounds or built entirely new stadia. However, I'm pleased to confirm that Wembley is still clearly without equal, as a shining example of what can be achieved when accountants aren't given the final say on prestigious and expensive projects being given the go-ahead.

If it is indeed accurate, the final reported spend of £798 million has to be considered a little self-indulgent, but having been able to bask in the warm glow of victory, watching my team win a play-off final at Wembley; I'd have to say it's money well spent.

The stunning 133-metre-high Wembley arch (seen in the background) is illuminated at night making the stadium visible for miles around. The warm glow lights up the North London sky, announcing to the world that the stadium is open for business.

It really doesn't matter if you're visiting Wembley for the first time or if you're making a return trip, you never tire of the overwhelming sense of occasion.

Decades of history and tradition add a vibrancy that flows through the 90,000 supporters, helping to make the visit a highly-charged experience.

Wembley is a thoroughly modern facility that easily caters for tens of thousands of spectators.

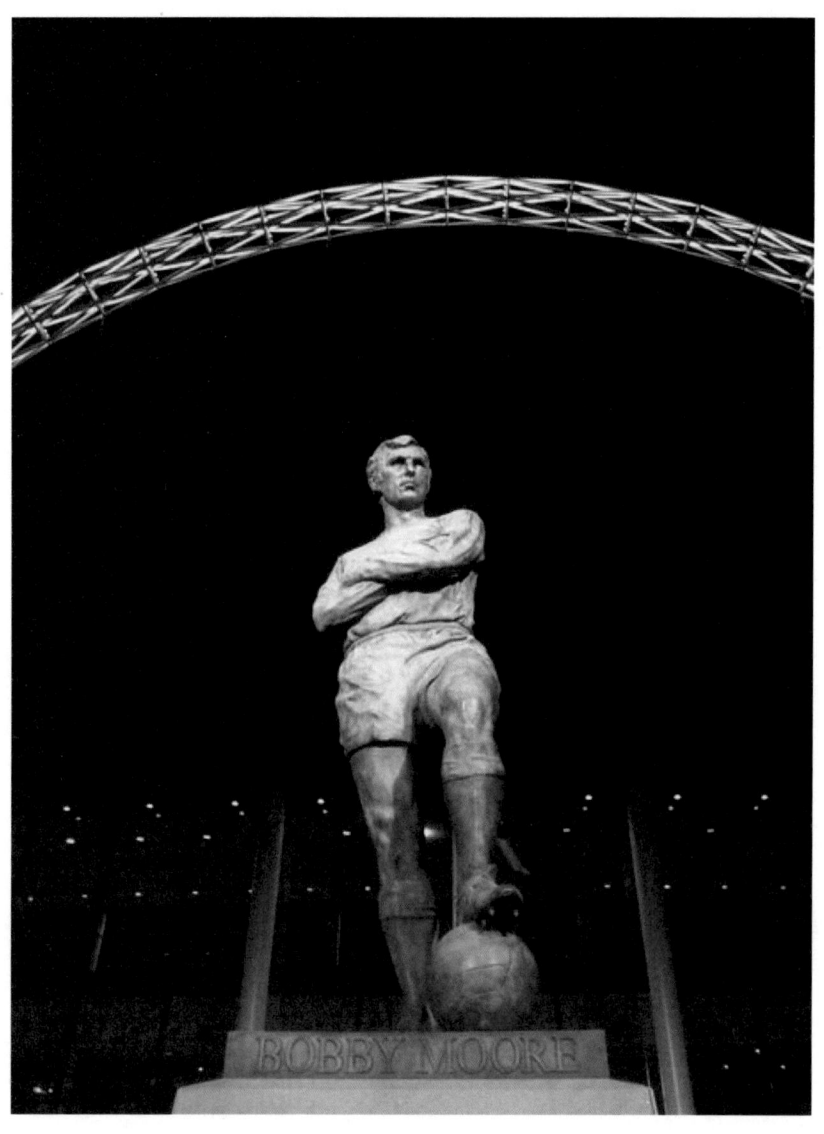

A 6.1-metre-high bronze statue of the late, great Bobby Moore sits outside the main entrance to the new Wembley stadium. A fitting tribute to the only Englishman ever to skipper his country to victory in a World Cup final. Such is the quality of the casting that in my opinion, the amazing detail gives you an indication of great man's personality. You can almost hear Bobby's voice telling the players and fans of visiting football teams from every nation across the world "If you want the ball, you're going to have to come and get it."

Photo by Chris Downer

When the stadium re-opened the FA oversaw the transition with little more than a whisper. A job well done in my opinion, a big, brash, opening ceremony would only serve to highlight the excessive cost of the rebuild.

It's difficult not to get drawn into a comparison with another new stadium being built 11 miles across London.

When compared to the FA's budget, the £390 million final cost of the new Arsenal stadium (the Emirates) has surely got to represent extraordinary value for money.

I understand the final cost of building the new Wembley Stadium was always going to be significantly more expensive, especially as the capacity at Wembley is 30,000 higher. However, sitting here with a pad, pencil and a calculator, I cannot get anywhere close to the reported final cost of building our new national stadium: £798 million.

MOST MEMORABLE MATCH

DERBY COUNTY 0 - 1 QPR
(SATURDAY 24TH MAY 2014)

QPR made their first appearance at the fabulous new home of English football in May of 2014. A two-legged, play-off semi-final victory against Wigan Athletic at the end of the 2013-2014 Championship campaign gave us the opportunity of returning to the Premiership at the first time of asking.

Despite the poor quality of the actual game itself, the Wembley final proved to be one of the most enjoyable and memorable occasions in all of my years of following QPR.

The ticket allocation for QPR fans had sold out well before the day of the game. We were fortunate enough to secure our tickets early, giving us plenty of time to go back and organise all of the trimmings required to make the day a huge success.

At 47 years of age, I'd like to say the day would be equally enjoyable if we went on to win or lose, however, life's not that simple. Despite the fact I am indeed old enough not to throw a tantrum if we had gone on to lose the game, it is true to say that defeat would have had a significant impact on the day.

From hiring a mini-bus, sorting out a venue for breakfast, to meeting up at Wembley with other members of the family, nothing was left to chance.

One of the party (Terry Cadby) had attended an unrelated celebratory event the previous evening. Sadly, being a helpless enthusiast when it comes to anything alcohol related he was 'running a bit late' the following morning. Unfortunately for the rest of our travelling party he was first on the list for collection. The tightly wound mini-bus driver (Lee Edmonds) was eager to stress the sense of urgency to our hungover Ranger at every possible opportunity.

As the mini-bus went to each of the collection points, the atmosphere became more and more diluted, and by the time we reached the M1 Motorway the chatter within the bus had returned to the normal mix of excitable QPR stories and mickey-taking.

Not that it really mattered but something none of us had considered is the majority of the 44,000 opposition supporters would be travelling down to London, using the same route as us!

Sitting in the mini-bus, the youngsters proudly wearing their blue and white hooped shirts and with flags and scarves hanging everywhere, we were instantly identifiable as QPR fans.

Looking back, I can't help but chuckle at the number of hand gestures coming from 99.9% of the Derby fans. One great example of different attitudes and behaviour from generation to generation came about from one of the many 5 seater coaches we passed on our journey. A Grandmother was sitting looking out of the window in between two younger sets of Derby fans, she was smiling and waving a genuine greeting to us, oblivious to the people sitting immediately in front and behind of her. I couldn't tell exactly what they were saying, although I believe they were under the impression we were employed in the money markets as bankers?

Our opponents, Derby County had been pushing for an automatic promotion place for months. Unfortunately, their challenge fell away towards the end of the season. They would eventually finish in third position, some eight points shy of second place. QPR finished the season in fourth place, five points behind Derby.

The final itself was a winner takes all affair, the victors banking a reported £134 million jackpot by earning the right to play in the following season's Premier League.

With so much at stake, it was perhaps no surprise that the match itself was full of tension and frustration. Yet again, QPR struggled to provide a performance worthy of a team favoured to gain promotion back to the Premiership when the season had kicked-off the previous August.

Over the 90 minutes Derby can certainly consider themselves really unfortunate not to have scored. Indeed, at times it almost seemed the match had descended into little more than shooting practice for the Midlands club.

All that was forgotten though, when seconds from the final whistle Bobby Zamora calmly slotted the ball past the despairing dive of the opposition's goalkeeper; our first and only effort on target throughout the entire match!

Certain goals are truly unforgettable for their craft, guile and skill. Bobby Zamora's winner was more of an instinctive finish though. Not that it matters, as his goal will live long in the memory of all QPR fans.

When the ball came to him after a determined run and cross from QPR's Junior Hoilett deep inside the Derby County penalty box, using his years of experience, he calmly guided the ball past the forlorn Derby goalkeeper.

For me, what made his goal so special was the almighty roar when he scored. The sense of relief at least doubled the volume of the celebrations.

The quality of the individual players was never in doubt, sadly though the team never matched the sum of its parts as QPR's form coughed and spluttered through the season.

The new Wembley stadium has a capacity of 90,000; when Zamora scored the QPR fans created an atmosphere of at least twice that number. Indeed, the noise of the celebration was so intense it sounded like a huge explosion, something that I'm assuming could be heard for miles around.

From the moment the ball left his boot, I was perfectly positioned to see nothing was going to prevent it from crossing the line.

What happened next is a curious reaction which I think is probably unique to fans of QPR. Even after the ball had clearly hit the back of the net, most QPR fans will have checked that the linesman's flag wasn't raised and that the referee had signalled a goal before we begin celebrating! Fortunately, the human brain works so quickly that from shot, to goal, through to our supporters celebrating almost appears to be a seamless sequence; I can promise you though a significant number of QPR fans will have checked before rejoicing!

CHAPTER 7
10ᵀᴴ MAY, 2015

Fewer than 12 months after our euphoric victory over Derby County in the Championship play-off final at Wembley, QPR were unceremoniously dumped out of the Premier League.

In no way should any QPR fan be remotely surprised, as in truth our performances through the 2014-15 season have been woefully short of the standard required to keep us in the top tier of English football.

Although I cannot speak for other fans, my hope is that in the clamour to return to the Premier League we don't again sell our soul, buying players with little or no interest in the club.

Certainly there was precious little sign of many of the team so easily beaten by Manchester City at the Etihad Stadium on the 10ᵗʰ May 2015 showing any pride in wearing their QPR shirt.

The final score of Manchester City 6 – 0 QPR was every bit as painful as the score line suggests. Oddly enough, it's not the margin of the defeat that sticks in my throat, it's the lack of anything close to a competitive performance that I'm finding it difficult to live with. I've spent most Sundays over the last few years watching my son Joshua play local junior football. I'm certain that if the boys in his team had put in performances as poor as the QPR team did at the Etihad they'd have been hauled off, the harsh words of the coach ringing in their ears.

Just to compound the misery, there are stories circulating that following our return to the football league that we'll be hit with a £60m fine for falling foul of the Football Association's financial fair play rules. Although the noises coming out of Loftus Road seem to suggest that we feel we have a case to fight these allegations, failure to pay the fine could lead to QPR being denied a place in the Championship.

That's the trouble with rollercoasters, not everyone can take the head spinning, stomach-churning excitement. I've long come to terms with the fact that I'm clearly a thrill seeker; I'm the one usually to be found at the front of the ride shouting "Come On You R'ssssss!"

EXTRA-TIME

Can you name the players in the 1979-80 team photo?

Back Row (left to right)
Micky Walsh, Martyn Busby, Ian Gillard, Bobby Hazell, Derek Richardson, Chris Woods, Peter Hucker, Steve Wicks, Glenn Roeder, Tony Curry, Stan Bowles.

Front Row (left to right)
Paul Goddard, Barry Wallace, Dean Neal, Clive Allen, David McCreery, Gary Waddock, Don Shanks.

QUIZ ANSWERS

1970s
1. 1974, Gordon Jago
2. 12
3. 8
4. Burnley
5. 1
6. Carlisle Utd.
7. Notts. Forest, Leyton Orient, Brentford
8. Tommy Docherty
9. Clive Allen
10. Clive Allen scored a hat trick

1980s
11. Holland Fly KLM
12. Clive and his brother Bradley
13. Besiktas
14. Leicester City and Wolves
15. Alan Harris
16. 1982
17. Birmingham City
18. Welsh
19. Tottenham Hotspur
20. Watford

1990s
21. Andy Sinton
22. Stuart Wardley
23. £2.35 million
24. Ray Harford
25. Everton
26. £1.5 million
27. Bolton, Manchester City
28. Dichio
29. (11)
30. Compaq

2000s
31. Lee Harper
32. (0-1) Gillingham, 20th February 2001
33. (2-0) Barnsley and Tranmere Rovers
34. Gulf Air
35. Garry Waddock
36. Huddersfield and Tranmere Rovers
37. Plymouth Argyle
38. Tommy Williams
39. (2 Points) QPR 83, Cardiff City 81
40. Wigan Athletic

2010s
41. Adel Taarabt
42. Adel Taarabt
43. (23) League Games
44. 17th
45. Ashley Young
46. 2-1
47. Gulf Air
48. Bolton, Blackburn and Wolves
49. Cardiff City
50. Barnsley, (4-0), Fitz Hall

MY 50ᵀᴴ BIRTHDAY SURPRISE

When the phone rang in the busy Ingram household in August 2016 I was a little annoyed that my whole family seemed to invite me to answer it. I was just about to sit down to eat my tea… bloody phone!

"Hello," I said in an impatient tone, obviously designed to knock whoever was calling me off their stride; it worked!

"Err, is that Simon?" Thinking it was a friend of mine I came within a whisker of telling him to p**s off as I was busy.

"Yes," I replied, in a get-on-with-it impatient voice. Now before anyone starts to build an image of me as a grumpy individual…I'm honestly not.

"You don't know who it is do you?" asked the man on the other end of the phone. *[Pause]* My mind spun at 100mph.

"It's Gerry Francis," for God's sake Gerry, why didn't you say so? My boyhood hero had contacted me to wish me a happy 50th birthday. It seems an odd thing to say but I did somehow recognise his voice. I guess after years of hearing him talk on TV you almost feel like you know famous people.

We chatted for about 30 minutes, all I can say is he's a fantastic fella. And yes, I did ask him what he considers to be the best goal he's ever scored (vs. Spurs) and what it was like to score a screamer against Scotland (he just laughed).

What I found most interesting was his very black-and-white recounting of his back injury in the mid-1970s. He couldn't walk properly so playing football was a physical impossibility. Without any noticeable anger in his voice, he talked about his injury and how it came so very close to ending his career. QPR had just finished a close second in the 1975-76 1st division campaign, he was captain of England; the world was full of opportunity.

All this changed so quickly, he was very philosophical…I'm still p****d off!

A huge thanks must go to Sharon Timms and Sue Williams for organising this fantastic surprise. They say that you should never meet your idol as you'll always be disappointed, it obviously doesn't apply to talking to them on the phone.